taj mahal

REVIEW

Cyberwit's International Journal
Devoted to Arts, Literature, Poetry &
Culture

Dr. Santosh Kumar

Editor

| VOLUME 20 | NUMBER 2 | DEC. 2020 |

Taj Mahal Review

www.tajmahalreview.com
Founded 2002

Taj Mahal Review is devoted to the cause of poetry so that our planet may be a better place to live in. What the Journal asks the poet is to be stimulated and moved by the visual and the aural imagery. The poems should reveal the remarkable variety of life, and a faith in life, blended by a healthy scepticism. The critical articles and essays should exhibit the post-modern trends, without obscurity, artificiality and violation of laws of criticism. Taj Mahal Review does not accept compositions founded on violent self-pity, or feelings of egocentricity. Poems, essays, literary articles, short stories, and book reviews are invited for publication in the International Journal Taj Mahal Review, published in June and December annually.

Editor

Dr. Santosh Kumar

Editorial Advisor

Maria Cristina Azcona
Ban'ya Natsuishi

Managing Editor

Dr. Karunesh Kumar Agrawal

Deputy Managing Editor

Radha Agrawal

Cyberwit.net, HIG 45, KAUSHAMBI KUNJ, KALINDIPURAM, ALLAHABAD - 211011 (U.P.) INDIA
www.cyberwit.net
www.facebook.com/pages/Allahabad-India/Cyberwitnet/178524375975
Tel: +(91) 9415091004

Subscription: Single Copy, Rs. 1000/-; $ 30
For subscribing please log on to www.tajmahalreview.com/subs.htm
E-mail: info@tajmahalreview.com

Taj Mahal Review is distributed by:

Amazon(USA, India)
Alibris (USA)
Cyberwit (India)
Flipkart (India)

MLBD Books International
D K Agencies (P) Ltd.
UBS Publisher's Distributors P. Ltd.
Nsi Infinium Global Pvt. Ltd.

ISBN: 978-93-88319-15-7

Typeset by Cyberwit.net.
Printed at THOMSON PRESS INDIA LTD.

How lucky, if they know their happiness,
Are farmers, more than lucky, they for whom,
Far from the clash of arms, the earth herself,
Most fair in dealing, freely lavishes
An easy livelihood.

- Virgil

You are my sun and stars, my night, my day,
My seasons, summer, winter, my sweet spring,
My autumn song, the church in which I pray,
My land and ocean, all that the earth can bring
Of glory and of sustenance, all that might be divine,
My alpha and my omega, and all that was ever mine.

- William Shakespeare

A writer, I think, is someone who pays attention to the world.

–Susan Sontag

Rats died in the street; men in their homes. And newspapers are concerned only with the street.

- Albert Camus

I can't think of a case where poems changed the world, but what they do is they change people's understanding of what's going on in the world.

- Seamus Heaney

I lost my center/ fighting the world

- Ezra Pound

POET GENE HIRSCH LEAVES BEHIND A MAGNUM OPUS

"SPEAK, SPEAK: POETRY BY GENE HIRSCH" By Gene Hirsch

Cyberwit.net Publishing

We often use the trope of a book as a metaphor for life, but what if we took this idea literally, composing a book over the arc of our lives: capturing, refining, and finally publishing our most profound experiences just as we reached our end? This is the inspired accomplishment of Dr. Gene Hirsch, whose collection of poems, "Speak, Speak: Poetry by Gene Hirsch" (edited by Judith Robinson) was published only weeks before he passed on Sept. 3 after a long battle with cancer. Dr. Hirsch was 88.

At 425 pages, "Speak, Speak" is a magnum opus, combining the energy of a Bildungsroman with the gravity of a memoir. It's Proustian in the clarity of its moments, yet Joycean in the sweep of its evolving consciousness. Dr. Hirsch specialized in geriatrics and was a noted authority on hospice education in Pittsburgh. His concern for suffering, and how we are impacted by death, infuses the 281 poems in this volume. He often employs a first-person personae — even when he reaches far beyond the boundaries of his own psyche — or the second-person, in works that empathically explore a multitude of lives, including prostitutes, transvestites, beggars, the blind, artists, and many other souls, both ancient and modern. For example, in the powerful "Blind Man" he asks:

"How did you find your way?
Did you kick the pebbles,
sense the soil and the berries,
smell the manure,
Hear the robins sing?"

For Dr. Hirsch, death, like life, is a journey not to be feared. In another poem that embodies this sentiment, "Finding His Way," he observes, "My friend has begun to die/ painfully shunning the call." He describes this person's crisis with a portentous metaphor, as "poppies, reduced to a liquor, / flux back and forth / through the worst of his pain." Eventually finding transcendence, the friend ". . . dreams of a well / in a parched field" then drops a stone, listening to the echo, until he becomes confident enough to lower himself down the rope, sings a song from his childhood, "and falls unceremoniously/ to the center of the Earth."

Dr. Hirsch achieves this kind of redemptive denouement in poem after poem without becoming maudlin, like a sanguine Virgil ushering us through a dark path to our own unknowable end.

One can detect influences in his work as varied as the surreal lyricism of James Wright, the eccentric inventiveness of Wallace Stevens, and the experimental forms of e.e. cummings. He also finds ekphrastic inspiration from composers such as Bach, and painters like Hieronymus Bosch. But as cosmopolitan as Dr. Hirsch is, his art is sui generis. As a critic once wrote of the French poet Paul Verlaine, "He may well have been influenced, for a moment, by some contemporary poets; but they merely awakened, merely revealed the extreme and painful sensibility which is his all."

Often the most striking accomplishments we discover in "Speak, Speak" are the moments of sublime expression, such as when the poet in "Who is Death?" offers the simile, "like tinctures of milt from craven satyrs" or declares, "Feed me your soul in delectable shades/ of rose petal dust." In "If you take nothing from these ramblings but" which comes near the end of the volume, we learn, "When oceans wash our earth / arks will preserve our intentions," which is biblical in its resonance.

Perhaps Dr. Hirsch's most illuminating revelation occurs during the introspective "In a Cup of Tea" when he states, "Silence is the economical way / to say everything at once." A conclusion, much like Hamlet's final utterance, that is a fitting summation of any poet's extraordinary lifelong journey.

https://www.cyberwit.net/publications/1477

Pittsburgh native Stuart Sheppard is a novelist, critic and technology management consultant. Twitter @HamletsMachine.

FROM THE EDITOR

The December 2020 issue of *Taj Mahal Review* presents some of the most attractive contemporary works by poets and creative artists across the world. I trust that readers who consider themselves interested in poetry, haiku and short story written by international authors, will agree that the latest journal includes not only quite attractive poetry, short story and book reviews, but also immortal haiku by poets across the globe. The poems and haiku selected for publication in this latest edition of TMR have a special interest as the most attractive images, sentiment, ideas and moods expressed by the poets undoubtedly reveal rare and precious quality of intense imagination and minute observation both suggestive and graphic.

It may be remembered that great poems are never rhetorical and declamatory in tone. The poets become immortal by their apt and quotable phrases as in these lines by John Milton revealing his great disappointment when he became blind:

Thus with the Year
Seasons return, but not to me returns
Day, or the sweet approach of Ev'n or Morn,
Or sight of vernal bloom, or Summer's rose,
Or flocks, or herds, or human face divine

But Milton grieves not and finds strength in the following lines:

So much the rather thou Celestial light
Shine inward, and the mind through all her powers
Irradiate, there plant eyes, all mist from thence
Purge and disperse, that I may see and tell
Of things invisible to mortal sight.

No doubt, the above incomparable quote reveals the sublime height and poignant intensity of Milton's poetry.

Congratulations to Louise Glück. The prestigious Nobel Prize in Literature 2020 was awarded to Louise Glück "for her unmistakable poetic voice that with austere beauty makes individual existence universal" The announcement was made on October 8, 2020. The following lines by Louise Glück are quite remarkable:

We respect, here in America / what is concrete, visible. We ask/ What is it for? - The Seven Ages

"The unsaid, for me, exerts great power..."

This is quite tragic and heartbreaking that during the COVID-19 pandemic, an increasingly large number of people died across the world. I along with Karunesh Kumar Agarwal and all staff members pray that God may grant peace and consolation to all bereaved families.

I would like to thank all the creative authors whose impressive writings are included in this latest TMR edition. I am highly obliged and grateful to all poets and short story writers for their kind cooperation and help to make publication of the journal possible. Happy New Year.

Best Wishes

SANTOSH KUMAR

Editor

CONTENTS

SHORT STORIES

SHORT ESSAYS

POEMS

HAIKU

REVIEWS

ARTS

American poet Louise Glück wins 2020 Nobel Prize for literature

STOCKHOLM — The Nobel Prize for literature was awarded to American poet Louise Glück on Thursday "for her unmistakable poetic voice that with austere beauty makes individual existence universal."

The prize was announced in Stockholm by Mats Malm, the permanent secretary of the Swedish Academy. Glück joins a handful of American poets who have received the prize, which has been dominated by novelists since the first award in 1901. She is also one of the few women honored — the 16th female Nobel Literature laureate.

Glück, who shuns most publicity, told Sweden's TT news agency from her home in Cambridge, Massachusetts, that her phone was ringing off the hook, and she was struggling to express her feelings about the award.

In a 2012 interview with the Academy of Achievement, Glück noted that "worldly honor makes existence in the world easier" but said he true goal as an artist was "not capable of being had in my lifetime."

"I want to live after I die, in that ancient way," she said. "And there's no way of knowing whether that will happen, and there will be no knowing, no matter how many blue ribbons have been plastered to my corpse."

In addition to being the recipient of myriad awards (among them the National Humanities Medal, Pulitzer Prize, National Book Award, National Critics Circle Award and the Bollingen Prize) Glück was the Poet Laureate of the Unites States from 2003 to 2004.

Glück, 77, who is a professor of English at Yale University, was born in New York and raised in a family with Hungarian Jewish origins. She has spoken of how a teenage struggle with anorexia, and the therapy she received for it, influenced her incisive writing.

A. McIntyre

THE TOY SHOP

Hey, come on in. The American beckoned, his teeth very white against a deep tan. We found the shop after a search of alleys in the old town north of the cathedral. He told us to visit, a message passed on by Pestañas. I wondered about his sense, running a toy shop in such an obscure part of town. But he knew what he was doing. He'd lived there for a long time.

How are you guys doing? Fine, I said, Fine. How about yourself? asked Gaz. Good, said the American, Just back from Texas. I told you I was traveling, didn't I? Well it was damn good to get out of this place for a while, gets to you. Know what you mean, muttered Gaz. He doesn't like it much, I said. Really? said the American, Trouble? Gaz nodded, Oh it's all right, takes a bit of getting used to. The American laughed, You're not the only one, different reality, different time. Mexican time. Too many Mexicaners for starters. Wish I could stay in Texas, but this place has its advantages. Anyway, come on in. He stared down the street at two men leaning against a wall. They grinned, one yelling, *Puto gringo*. He waved, Friends of mine, a couple of guys who work for me now and then. We entered the shop.

Here it is, this is it. He pointed vaguely. Wait here, hey sit down. I'll be right back. He disappeared into the back of the store through a mesh curtain of colored beads. I looked at the garish walls. A chandelier hanging above us. Hundreds of toys lining the shelves, steel chess sets, designer clocks, bright contraptions, steel decorations. I wondered how he made any money. I looked at Gaz, and he raised his eyebrows. All right, like I said, here we go, yelled the American returning with a rolled newspaper. We were sitting at a glass table in the middle of the room. Some people tried the door, a couple shopping. We're closed, shouted the American, Go away. The couple ambled on.

The American unrolled the newspaper revealing clumps and fronds of fresh marijuana. An odor of fermenting mint and newly mown lawn. He began to roll a Havana. This stuff is all right, he whispered, Not bad, it'll do, but tomorrow if you guys are around I'm going to get some more from someone I know, much better. This here weed is average. Bought it last week, and it's reasonable. Nothing special though. He lit the joint, inhaling twice, his head disappearing in a cloud. He passed the smoldering cigar to Gaz. Gaz puffed, coughing, handing it to me. I sucked, the cigar crackling like a bonfire, one more time, gagging, giving it to the American. He motioned to Gaz. Gaz shook his head, grinning vacantly, his eyes already glazed red. If this is average, I dunno what good is, he droned, his nasal Liverpool accent making us laugh. I'm all right too, I agreed, chuckling, Bloody good stuff, very strong actually. The American deposited the cigar in a huge conch shell that served as an ashtray. The room buzzing. About half the joint remained, the paper stained black from the tar. Some music, he announced, rolling his chair backwards. He switched on a system by the wall. Yoko Ono.

So how've you guys been? Oh, not much happening, I replied, Not much to report. The American smiled, No news is good news, is what I say. I got this album in Japan, Plastic Ono. You were in Japan? I asked. The American smiled, Yeah, a while ago, when I was in the Army. When did you leave? Gaz mumbled. The Army? Oh, about five years ago. Before that I was in Germany, before that was Nam. Gaz leaned forward, You were in Vietnam? The American lit a Marlboro, Yeah. Two tours. Long time ago, he added, exhaling a stream of smoke, Long time. So now you run a shop, I said. The American began to laugh uncontrollably. Did he say something? asked Gaz grinning. For a moment, I thought the American was crying. The shop, he chuckled finally, his eyes red streaming tears, The shop, those two sad fucking tourists. Bet you boys think this shop is weird. A bit, I agreed. The American pointed at a yellow spaceship alarm clock, I mean, who buys that, who the fuck would ever buy a piece of crap like that? He began to laugh again, tears running down his face. Then suddenly he was serious, his face deadpan. He stubbed the cigarette, his eyes narrowing. He wiped his face, And who gives a shit? It doesn't matter. No-one comes here, ever, and why the fuck should they? Those two idiots just now are the first people who wanted to come here in over a month, maybe two, I don't fucking know, I don't give a fucking damn either. They were probably from California, where the fuck else would they be from? This place is appearances, impressions, is all. He lit another cigarette, I know you boys won't talk, and it doesn't matter if you do, I really don't give a shit. I mean who the fuck are you going to talk to? I work for the Governor. Train the body guard, teach them how to shoot, that kind of thing, get them fit for duty. I'm an advisor. Interesting, I said. Oh, you know, it's slack, continued the American, Real slack, just a bit of fun, a fucking holiday, and I get paid. Title's Special Advisor, a bunch of crap. Only thing special about it is they pay me dollars and I do fuck all. Easiest work I ever did. Fucking siesta. The whole thing's a fucking game. Ever thought about that? Nothing to do. Take my boys out now and then into the mountains, let them blaze away with their guns, teach them how to fight, that sort of thing. Make 'em happy. They love noise. Nothing to it. I get a lot of free time. They're good boys, but you need to push them. And they need us here, man, they'd fucking fall apart without us, whole country would go down the fucking tube, it's just a step away, fucking funny farm. What was it Porfirio Diaz said? Poor little Mexico, so far from God, so near to the USA. Well, you know what? God ain't there and the USA is. Dig that. God bless America. Here the fuck we are, and we ain't going anywhere. Know what I mean?

Someone was knocking on the glass door. I looked round. A tall cadaverous Mexican youth grinning, standing in the entrance. Ramon, said the American. He stood up, leaned towards the door, and let the fellow in. Ramon, some friends, the American announced in Spanish. This boy's as dumb as a bastard, he added in English, But he's a good old boy aren't you Ramon. The youth grinned vacantly, not understanding. We acknowledged him. The American began to talk in dialect, something about tomorrow, a *rollo*, midday. The youth nodded. They shook hands, the Mexican waving as he left. The American shut the door, Did you see the size of his hands? Yeah, replied Gaz laughing, His hands. I noticed the hands, but I thought it was the marijuana. The American chuckled, Biggest hands you'll ever see, he should learn the piano. He's going to bring me another one of these tomorrow. The American indicated the newspaper. Best fucking news I ever had. But better, he emphasized, whistling, Much better. One toke stuff, absolutely kickass. Give you guys some, if you show. He sat down.

Yup, I'm the most useful guy you're likely to know in this here town, the back of beyond, the real boonies down here, fucking nowhere, you know what I mean. Out in the fucking badlands. Don't know what I'm doing here sometimes. I mean have you ever thought, where the fuck are we? What the fuck are we doing here? Used to be much worse though, a few years back. Cleaned the place up. But seriously, one sign of trouble, from anyone, you boys come see me, is that clear? Ain't having nobody push around a couple of good boys like you, 'coz good boys is what you are, I can see that. Thanks, I said, Appreciate it, I hope it won't be necessary. Gaz nodded, Yeah, thanks a ton. You never know, said the American, Just in case. It's good to have, that's the way it works down here. I'll help you out. If you can't find me go see Manuel. You know Manuel? No, I replied. The American motioned, The big fellow at the cafe, always with me, he's Manuel. Strong bastard. Once saw him kick the shit out of five guys. Any problems, if I'm not around, go see him. He'll help you out too, just say you know me. He's useful. Thanks, I repeated. Yeah, thanks, said Gaz. The American shook his fist, That's the way it works here, rules're simple. Like I told you once before. We work together. Big stick. *Mucho palo.* There's nothing else. That's why this country's so goddamn simple. I'm only telling you boys this 'coz you're white. Least you ain't fucking Mexicaners. Know what I mean? We're in this together. And just to let you know I'm serious, I mean business, I'm not fucking around, look here at this. The American reached into his jacket, pulling out a revolver, a .38 by the look of it. He smiled, The look on you boys faces, what do you expect? I'm from Texas. Texas godammit. I had a great granddaddy in the Texas Rangers for Chrissakes. Scares the shit out of them if you wave that.

He placed the gun on the table next to the newspaper. No-one's going to fuck with you, now you know James R. McKechnie III. That's me. He held the joint and lit it, inhaling, holding the smoke. He passed it to Gaz. I declined when Gaz was done, I'm really stoned, couldn't handle any more, it's like standing over a chimney. I got there a while back, mumbled Gaz, Too much. So we'll meet tomorrow? the American asked. Sure, I replied. Yeah, why not? agreed Gaz. Good, then that's settled. You guys ever eaten fresh *duraznos* straight from the tree? I looked at Gaz, Can't say we have, you ever eaten *duraznos*? *Duraznos*? said Gaz. The American pointed vaguely, Tomorrow we'll go to the jungle and find some. Nectar of the gods, fruit of the country, a reason to live, like eating a woman. *Duraznos.* I know where some is. I've got a couple of days off. There's an old deserted farm way out there with trees. We'll take some of this stuff and go. I'll show you around. Sounds good, I said, So here tomorrow about midday? The American nodded, Yeah, midday. We stood up unsteadily and shook hands. Yoko Ono screaming. It was already dark. Well, *hasta luego amigos*, drawled the American, Good of you boys to come by. Good to see some white boys in town after so long. Kinda gets to you, know what I mean? Gotta stick together. Hey, thanks for everything, I said. Yeah, thanks repeated Gaz. We waved and the American shut the door. The town spread across the hillside in the distance, points of light in the dark, the vast darkness of the jungle beyond. The men we had seen earlier were still there. One of them yelled, *Puto, puto gringo, gringo cabron.* Ignoring them, we walked away. Looks like a model, said Gaz, Like a model railway or something. Yeah, I agreed, A cartoon, not quite real, like those paintings done with dots.

Fran Shaw

HEADS UP

High in the Swiss Alps, at the front of a great hall filled with seekers, LeClair asks, "Who here thinks they have a reliable mind?"

The four people most lost in thought raise their hands. That's how Dan sees it. After decades of these summer retreats, he knows what the takeaway will be—"You are not what you think"—but wonders when he'll feel the truth of it.

The task for the four volunteers is to report at dinner everything said now at lunch. The question under discussion: What is the relationship between knowledge, being, and understanding?

Dan has been hauling boulders all morning and wants to nap. Various people give their views. Elegant concepts. Articulate theories. Dan wishes he could press the MUTE button.

"The awakened mind is...."

All in the head. Full of ideas. The bait is not the fish!

"We are powerless when it comes to...."

You don't know what you're talking about.

"...my nothingness in the face of the great Unknown."

Even the known is unknown.

One-upping every speaker like this...old thought form... feels wrong. *Just listen*, he tells himself. *Others experience the world differently.* But when will it not be just theoretical, divine Love, unconditioned joy—annoying to hear spoken about when one is struggling. Dan turns away to watch giant puffed-up clouds stream by the window. *A chalet in the clouds—*

"Dan," comes the voice from the front of the room. LeClair asks, "Do you know the saying that begins 'All men are dead'?"

"Uh… not sure."

"It's from the 12th century Sufi, Dzou'l Noun." LeClair recites slowly— as the volunteers lean in—

"All men are dead except those who know.

All men who know are dead except those who practice.

All men who practice are dead except those who act with right intention.

And all those who act with right intention are in very grave danger."

Grave danger. Said with a twinkle in the eye, but Dan feels the truth of it. *Lord, help me be aware enough to know I'm not awake.*

At dinner the volunteers report what was said at lunch. No two accounts are alike. The words have fallen differently on the different types.

"So this is a reliable mind," says LeClair.

More discussion. *We're professionals at this.*

LeClair teases, "Your answers give the illusion of being intelligent."

"What's frustrating," Dan speaks up, "is coming into a state in which I understand better what's taking place, and then in the next moment I don't, but act as if I do. What is the proper role of the head?" *You'll go far listening to me.*

"Instead of my mind-dominated usual condition, my wavering state," says LeClair, "with an active attention—sensing the body, the feelings join, the force equally in all parts—something refined can penetrate."

No one speaks.

LeClair continues, "When very quiet inside—need an atmosphere of sensitivity—aware of breathing—this Intelligence appears, deep intelligence. If the mind starts to think about this or that, not necessary now, let it go. I don't want to lose contact with this Intelligence because it's precious, so I return, not to grasp at it—not imagination and thought—but a very active attention." The sparkliness in the room doubles. "Thinking breaks the charm."

It's the first time Dan hears the word *intelligence* with what sounds like a capital *I*. An Intelligence that bypasses thought? Clearly, it's not the voice-in-the-head that says, "I get it and you don't." *Lord, help me to be conscious.*

LeClair asks Dan to take charge of the entertainment for the last-night celebration. A U.S. sitcom T.V. veteran, Dan has helped LeClair in this way many times. There is such a warm feeling between them because with Dan there is no pretense and always a funny comment. But what to do this week that hasn't been done before?

Inspiration comes at dinner as people tell stories, a rite of passage for newbies if they want to get invited back. Some of the tales this year are quirky. A Native American gentleman brags about his tribe's "extraordinary ability always to know which direction we're facing." LeClair blindfolds him, spins him around, and asks which direction, but the man can't get it right. Dan knows the feeling. Where's the compass? Where true north?

Dessert is served—but the ice cream sits melting in the bowls while everyone is forced to listen to "Woody, the Remarkable Dog." Woody's owner, the misguided teller of All Tales Woody, never once refers to Woody with a pronoun but repeats the name—for the hundredth Woody time!

LeClair comments, "You are never to do that again."

Everyone eats dessert. The woman next to Dan is annoyed. "Sorry you had to listen to my husband go on and on about losing his dog. All day long for years he was all sweetness with the dog, 'Oh, puppy, puppy.' But when he talks to *me*, it's always, 'What? Are you nuts?'" She sighs. "I guess I'm just glad something made him that cheery for that long." She points to the dessert in the bowl. "Can you tell what it is?"

Dan assesses the swirly liquid with the dark chunks. "Chocolate soup?"

"It *was* ice cream with pears and chocolate sauce. We served 90 portions at the last possible minute to keep it cold, and everyone was about to taste it when we were forced to listen to that dog story. Next time I'll bake a cake."

"Yes, all the sad tales," says Dan. "I didn't realize I was so happy."

"Got any aspirin?"

"Maybe we should put it on the cake."

People and their stories. *Could be funny*, the 1001 things we get identified with, the ego displays, all of it so plain to see (in others, of course). Switch it up a bit? Play it for laughs?

By week's end Dan and friends have prepared skits in hats culminating in a rambling tale made of the week's best bits. His arms hidden, Dan delivers the monologue as Professor Snellby while a friend behind him does the arms, making funny hand gestures as commentary. "Let me tell you about the Unknown." The performance, a hit. *It's so great to see LeClair laugh.*

The next morning, at the last meal before people return home, Dan sits cross-legged on a cushion in the first row facing LeClair who is saying, "How to develop sustained attention? Be passionate about it. 'Passionating' in it."

Dan smiles. For a moment it is like lying on the beach in the sun and everything is okay. Such a relief after a lifetime trying to control it all. The sole urgency now: attending second by second this Light; there is no next moment.

He starts to eat his scrambled eggs when—suddenly—of all things—

He gets up and goes to his dorm. When he returns, he encounters a silence so deep that his feet scurfing along the floor make the only sound.

He is about to sit down when LeClair looks up at him.

Dan waits a beat, then says, "I forgot my teeth."

Laughter. The room explodes with it. Yes, it is funny. And he plays it for laughs. But right away he feels bad. *A smartass comment at the wrong moment.* Back in his seat, he looks down at his eggs, cold on the plate.

All morning he thinks: a sacred moment, the culmination of the week's work, and *I stepped on it.* He locates LeClair supervising the dismantling of the large tent that was the men's dorm.

Dan apologizes. "I'm sorry about breakfast. I ruined the moment. All together in that wonderful silence—"

"No, no. You got me off the hook."

"How hard it is to use the head in the right way."

"Come for tea later and we'll talk."

Six men shoulder a heavy pallet that was the tent floor and carry it up the incline. Dan walks quickly toward them to help. Just as he reaches them, they stop short—

Whack! A metal edge gets him. He's down. Blood trickles from the gash on his forehead. Two doctors come quickly. The eye is okay—lucky. They clean the wound. But how to close it? Stitch it?

LeClair arrives, examines the cut, and puts a Band-Aid on it. He says to Dan, *so funny and sweet*, "This is not the right way to use your head." LeClair sits down next to him.

Dan feels like the sleepy Zen novice newly conked on the noggin by the "head" monk to wake up.

"How do you feel?" says LeClair.

Dan only nods; thoughts knocked right out of him. He's watching two women hang pillowcases on the clothesline. Bend, step, reach; bend, step, reach; a dance. The meadow in sunlight; the women moving in the quiet; the atmosphere around them, him; what bliss.

"So it's not about figuring out anything," Dan says finally, "when I'm lucky enough to direct connectly.*" Direct connectly?* He chuckles. "I can't think and I can't speak."

"Why don't you start a group when you get home," LeClair surprises him. "Maybe you already know someone who's interested."

"I'm no teacher." Dan has looked beneath the golden robes of the spiritually well-endowed. *Grave danger.* "My ego would get a little too involved. It thinks it's a competition."

"There is a need for something to pass, to circulate. The Light, moving always through everything. No ideas about it."

"But people want to discuss ideas. I used to. Can't stuff that turkey anymore."

"When the fish is caught, throw away the net."

"Good to hear. When I'm like this—very focused, very concentrated— I understand what you say." Dan smiles. "But the fish is slippery. I can go on talking as if I'm serving Something that I'm not actually aware of anymore." He stops. "That's what the head is for? To monitor that, so there's a coming back?"

"The calling back of the attention has awakening power," says LeClair. "Not to confuse the one who thinks with the one who is aligned. When you are dispersed, let the Attention touch your state. Just be sure you're really letting the contact appear. See the power in you." We have greater capacity than we know!

A movement from above makes Dan look up. Blackbirds swooping in the high currents. Treetops swaying, each in its own tempo, yet all of one motion. The wavering compass steadies, oriented to a new possibility.

"It's like the mind has stepped aside," says Dan. "I hear yo, but right now none of it starts up thoughts. This other quality that's here… needs everything, every bit of attention every second, to stay joined with it. That is how it feels."

"It is the state of not being taken. When the energy comes through, it is a taste of freedom—no mind—and when you are connected with that, you don't have to pretend."

"And what about always wanting to point out where someone else is going astray?"

LeClair turns to him so they are eye to eye. "That is because you still think it's yours, this experience. Like a little bit of carpet that needs to have a speck taken off. You think it belongs to you. There is no *you*. It is complete identification. Either one is identified with the body or one is in this flow, the true Self."

Michael J. Shepley

SECRET AGENT MAN

- Let me get this straight. You want me to fly over there?

- Yes.

- And get sick. With…

- Covid.

 Silence

- Sounds like you have an understanding of the basic parameters of the mission.

- Are you insane?

 Silence

- Ummm, you know we're not all that much into the rank thing here, being ostensibly a civilian operation, but… a little respect for elders and betters.

- Sorry. But why should I commit suicide?

- Well… at your age it'll be now worse than a bad cold. Probably. By the numbers.

 Silence

- And then there is the 25,000. Combat pay, so to say.

- You could have started there…

- Yes, of course… but are you listening now?

secret agent   2/5

- For the sake of argument, lets us say yes…

- Second: the bug has undergone a change. Evolution, it would seem. Reports have the new variant as more aggressive with respect to infection, but far less fatal.

- How far less?

- Way way. Like one tenth the original.

- Huh. Hadn't heard that. Still, what the point of sending anyone, namely me, to go and get infected?

- Huhhuhhuh… clearly so we can get the bug back here and isolate it in a lab.

- Why not just ask them over there for the damn thing?

   Cold comes the reply

- Don't you think we did that? First? Many times? They are just way too busy fighting the first bug to bother separating out the second. Lives at stake and all that rubbish. Or…

- Or?

- Or that's just what they're telling us.

- Huh.

- Indeed, a big HUH, huh? Our good mates.

- So, again, what's the big deal? With getting the second virus?

   Silence

- Can't you work that out? Pretty simple idea, really.

- End to the games. Just spill the beans. I know what our business is, so don't try to gas me. Give me the real story.

- A bit beyond your pay grade, I am afraid.

- Fine. Toodleloo.

secret agent   3/5

- Wait. Ok, when we have it we will clone it. See?

- I am not an idiot. I KNOW we are going to clone it. So what?

- And then…

- THEN?!!

- Disseminate it, naturally.

- What the hell…

- Look. There are all sorts of fire similes used describing the pandemic. Embers. Flare ups. Brushfire. In that vein, we are going to set a backfire.

- Backfire?

- Burn up all the fuel before the real wall of flame arrives.

    Silence

- So, if everyone were to get the second bug first…

- Ayre ya go. Knew you had a brain.

- It's to inoculate, a sort of vaccine…

- Ta Da! Care to go for extra credit, given the business you are in?

- I'm a biologist. With a PhD.

- Your title is epidemiologist. Level II. And we paid for your PhD.

- Yah, well…

- Yah well… you owe us. Big. Formally, the people of the realm. But why dither over fine points, eh?

- Yah well, you have to tell me HOW you intend to disseminate the new bug I am supposed to sneak back home. After you multiply it…

    Silence

secret agent   4/5

- Come to think, how are you going to multiply it? Quick. In test tubes?

    Coldly again

- Not your concern.

- Right.

    Silence

- Ahhh, look. This is urgency. We may be under a Bioweapon attack.

- What? How's that work?

- Think again. Work that grey matter. Killer pathogen. Appears suddenly. Out of who knows where.

Tens of thousands dropping. Horribly. Bleeding in the lungs. Then, magically, in one place, a second version crops up. Vaccinating the populace, so to speak. What great luck, eh? Nice and natural looking.

No fingerprints.

- You CAN NOT really believe that fantasy scifi conspiracy theory.

- We are paid to tackle wild and crazy events. The hypothesis fits facts.

It is entirely, technologically, possible. And surely, no one would unleash such a weapon without having the anti-dote.

- That the Chinese…

- Who says them? Why would they whack themselves to start the ball rolling. More like they were the target. Worst timing for an infectious outbreak. Their biggest travel holiday. Universal contagion.

- But there is no evidence of cloning. No sign of engineering. No crspr.

- Now, biologist, how have humans cultivated genetics fro the past centuries, even before they knew what a gene was? Cows, pig, dogs, maize, wheat, rice, you name it. All "engineered". Just a slower process. But, again, no fingerprints. No crspr. But far from impossible.

- By whom?

secret agent   5/5

- Isn't that a good question. But we have to survive the what is to ever get to answer that.

Silence

- What's this?

- A packet of tests. With luck we can sneak you back on commercial air before you show symptoms.

If not, we have other ways…

Silence

- Alright, I get it. Except… I have to know. How are you going to disseminate it once I bring it back, and you isolate the damned thing?

Silence

Silence

- Quit messing around in the desk drawers.

- I know… it is in here… somewhere… shiny, military… NATO caliber…

- Very amusing.

Silence

- Truth or consequences time, my young friend. Are you going? Or not?

Prof. Moshé Liba

THE MANY UNPROMISED LANDS

In my farewell speech from Miami, Florida (1993), I included this definition: "To be a diplomat is difficult. To be a Jewish diplomat is tenfold difficult. It is to live with antisemitism, with antizionism, to meet your enemies with a glass of drink in your hand. It is to be unique, different..."

Indeed, different, the Israeli diplomat is an envoy in search of Jews, or at least after remnant signs of Jews and Jewishness in the past, someone who often contributes to preserve the Jewish identity.

An Israeli diplomat is another kind of wandering Jew, before, during and after his diplomatic service. During my long diplomatic service, I came across many traces of Jews in the past, to discover from the Jewish history in remote places, I could help to bring them to the light, by organizing events and through my writings.

As a child, I listened to songs yearning to Jerusalem, to the Promised Land - Eretz Israel, occasionally sang for me by my mother. I heard in the synagogues and at the Pessach Seder the prayers: Next year in Jerusalem! But I heard also in the street, the shouting against me: Jews to Madagascar! As a youngster, I followed the wishes of the youth movements: To Palestine – Eretz Israel!

When I became a diplomat, I heard, I met with, I saw the traces of Jewish presence.

From the very first ceremonies of presentation of credentials as Ambassador to Presidents, some of them took advantage of our meetings to proudly mention the Jewish point of their country.

President Léopold Sédar Senghor of Senegal leaned back during the meeting and said: "My name Senghor comes from the Portuguese Senior, which is a Jewish name, and so were my ancestors."

Senghor recommended to go to the IFAN – Institut Fondamental d'Afrique Noire, where a research was done on the Jewish presence sur "La Petite Côte" after the 1492 expulsion of Jews from Spain and later from Portugal. President Ferrier of Suriname offered me after the ceremony of presentation of credentials the choice: a trip to the Saramacca where it was proposed to settle a Jewish region, or a trip to more ancient Joden Savanne, where Jews originally from the expulsion of

Spain and Portugal arrived, after having settled in Brazil.

While in Australia, I was welcomed by the Governor of West Australia with the story of a project to settle Jews in Kimberley: "you might have been now one of my citizens". The Governor of Tasmania received me with the story of a similar project in his island.

Miguel Trovoada, the President of São Tomé and Principe talked to me about the 2000 Jewish child slaves who were sent from Lisbon by the King of Portugal in order to convert them to Christianity, to marry them with slaves brought from Angola in Africa, and so to create a new race as the settlers of São Tomé.

I first heard the story of Sosúa, a safe haven for Jews, from the Ambassador of Santo Domingo, Dominican Republic in Israel, when I was Director General of the Central Institute of Cultural Relations in Jerusalem. He proudly told me that his country was the only offering to receive Jews from the Holocaust – by implementing at Sosúa the modest project of saving Jews from Europe.

These are only examples of the lands and places where there were projects of settling the Jews as part of the solution, a saving possibility from the Nazi "Final solution".

The denomination of "Unpromised Lands" was coined by Leon Gettler in his book: An Unpromised Land, Fremantle Arts Center, Perth, 1993. There were many others: Tasmania, Jewish Homeland, A Jewish State in America, An Autonomous Region in Russia /URSS – A re-settlement of Refugees from Europe Birobidzhan, A safe Haven for Jews, A New Jerusalem, A Jewish Community in Saramacca, Joden Savanne.

It is not easy to present in an article: the Uganda project, debated and finally rejected by the Zionist Movement at its very beginnings; Birobidzhan, the Russian region in URSS, established by Stalin; and not the Jewish agricultural region established in Argentina by The Baron Hirsch; and we still have mentioned the activity of non - Zionist movements looking for a solution to the Jewish settlement outside the Land of Israel, actually the real non – Promised Lands. The most active organization was the Freeland League called also the Territorialists, besides Australia and Suriname, also the French Colonies, French Guyana, British Guyana, and more, they pursued Jewish settlements in countries like Canada, Libia, Angola.

Over the years, I dealt with these projects in different ways: articles, international conferences, books, project of a film, and intend to present them in a book.

In the process of "resettlement", and due to the existence of a "British Mandate in Palestine E.I.", new camps were raised in places like Mauritius and Cyprus, they were not the promised lands and Madagascar was also not the Unpromised Land.

After the Holocaust in Romania/Transnistria, I made my way as an illegal immigrant across the Danube to Bulgaria boarding at the Burgos port the immigrants' ships of Pan Crescent and Pan York. We sailed on the Black Sea to the Dardanelles and on the Mediterranean Sea, only to be stopped by British war navies and imprisoned in the camps of Cyprus for a year. It was not another Unpromised Land, there were other camps after the Holocaust.

There are also communities like in Africa that reclaim descendants from Jews:

Beta Isra¬el – Ethiopia; Ibo – Nigeria; Jews luso – Africans – Cap-Vert; Lemba – Zimbabwe; Lemba – South Africa; Sefwi – Ghana; Tutsi – Rwanda; B'nai Ephraim (fils d'Ephraim) – Yoruba, Nigeria; Gnawa – Tombouctou; and others.

There are also towns which were called "Little Jerusalem's" in different countries. Here we bring an example from Italy.

La Piccola Gerusalemme, Gli Ebrei a Pitigliano.

Entrada a la "Piccola Gerusalemme", (la Chika Yerushalayin), at kuartier djudio restorado de Pitiliano

To Pitiliano – La Chika Yerushalayim al Sud de Toscana, we will dedicate another article.

Prof. Moshé Liba, 2020

Nina Rubinstein Alonso

BALANCING ON ONE LEG

Pays the vendor, wraps roasted peanuts in her green scarf, walks by cows, opens the heavy door to the windowless basement office, hotter than yesterday, but power's back on, ceiling fan moving, computer slow to reboot.

Last week she sent project photos of bags hand-woven from recycled fabrics, the dhobi scrubbing laundry by the river, the rickshaw wallah at the station, the plumbing shop's stack of white toilets, to give Global XPress a feeling for the village. She's cracking peanuts in a low budget office, nothing like glossy magazines where India glows gold and saffron, red wedding silk, ripples ochre and magenta, pungent spices, the Taj Mahal.

"Heard anything, Jessie? Don't expect much though the cooperative helps lower caste widows and survivors of forced prostitution. Been here five years, that's how it goes," Harris, wiping sweat off his glasses.

Last year she won an internship at a New York art gallery, planned to share an apartment with two friends, but Kara emailed from Vermont, "I'm rather pregnant," later sent snapshots of her pink-faced newborn with a note, "Busy with baby, work and Dan, not into getting married."

Then Lauren called saying her editing job came through at the Boston branch of Global XPress, not New York, adding, "I'm in a relationship with a woman. A friend since grade school just put me on her lesbian shit list."

"My brother Josh came out in high school. No idea how you'd take it, so kept quiet."

"Figures," Lauren sighs.

Then the gallery encounters a funding crunch, Jessie left with no internship, no room-mates, stuck in her childhood bedroom in western Mass. with her widowed mom and brother Josh, working at an ice-cream shop while designing video-games in his bedroom.

The India project post is on the university site, and she applies thinking, 'What the hell?' The offer arrives, and she jumps.

"Doubt more photos will help." He's squinting through foggy glasses, irritable since next year's funding, usually set by now, is up in the air. They sleep together off and on and off.

Lauren's email: "Sorry, can't include Hand-loom Artisan Cooperative this issue of Global XPress, so many NGO's, acute need everywhere. The editors chose a medical facility in Mumbai getting coverage for their orphaned children's school. But I've attached list of university job postings, one nearby at Vision International, take a look." She's included a video clip of a human-rights activist and a financial industry billionaire handing checks to the Mumbai facility's director, cameras clicking.

Harris: "Celebrities performing tax-deductible good deeds, flashy media hype, and we get shit."

July, in DC for medical check ups and visa updates, they receive official word that funding for Hand-Loom Artisan Cooperative is on indefinite hold.

"After five years with a golden track record? What the fuck?"

Needing work, Jessie applies to Vision International, knowing nothing about it. An offer arrives, lousy money, but she takes it.

"Vision International? Academia?" Harris taught at a Pennsylvania college, "Lectured note-taking muffins, endured boring faculty meetings, committee claptrap, hypocritical politics, dead end gig."

His book on micro-economics was reviewed as 'insightful, fine-tuned,' but didn't deliver tenure as the committee deemed Harris 'thorny, difficult to work with,' and hired someone else.

"Give me beltway bandits any day," what Harris calls D.C. consulting groups. "I know where they're coming from, everyone competing for grants and contracts, no phony smiles as if you're a dear colleague. At the university it started out buddy-buddy but I got kicked in the ass, project co-opted, one grant application rejected, the next taken over by the department head who treated me like a dumb ass."

Her contract arrives, and she signs via computer. Sharing the summer sublet with him has gone from awkward to uncomfortable to unbearable. The night before he leaves for New York seeking alternate funding, he's smashing plates.

"You're screwing me over, ditching me, and don't say you need your fucking woman space."

Angry, can't listen, talking to him is useless. She retreats to the bedroom, packed suitcases hidden in the closet, hears him sweeping broken glass, glad she didn't tell him she's rented a car and is leaving as soon as he's out the door.

Three a.m. he's opening drawers, looking for something, getting ready for his red-eye flight. Awake, she's unsure what to do if he kisses her neck, tries to make up, but he doesn't, goes back to the living room couch.

The front door finally slams. She listens to be sure he's not coming back, pulls on jeans and a t-shirt, drops a note on his computer, drags suitcases, a small fan, a rolled up foam mattress, statue of Ganesh (remover of obstacles) and a potted fern to the elevator then the rental car. Ten hours blasting pop music so she won't doze and drive off the road.

She's signed a twelve month contract for a staff position in international project development, requested India, but could get stuck doing data entry at a computer in a stateside office. She's nobody special, one article in a small journal, so who knows what she's in for?

Highland Ave., Somerville, she finds a sealed envelope in the mailbox with the realtor's note, keys and a coded confirmation number to call. She walks the stuffy third-floor space, leaves the required message, no idea when her roommate, found on line, will arrive. Can't budge the newly painted kitchen window, but shoves one open in the narrow living room then pulls the porch door wide, though there's no breeze. No lizards chasing bugs on the ceiling, no need to put mothballs in the sink the way they did in India to step critters crawling up the drain.

She's rubbing ice on her headache, staring at the fern she dropped, dirt and cracked pottery, hears someone on the stairs, tosses ice in the sink, wipes her hands on her jeans.

An Asian woman. "Kim?"

"Jessie? An attic?" Kim, sky blue purse over her shoulder, squints at the angled ceiling. "Good thing we're not six-footers. Which room or don't you care?"

"The one by the porch, olive walls I'll paint. Sorry about the mess, no broom."

Stepping over the dirt, "Hope the other room's bigger as I have a work table."

"It is. India last year, no furniture."

"Gave a nice bureau to my friend Nick, left junk on the LA sidewalk, no sense shipping a wine-stained, cat-scratched sofa cross country." Kim takes in Jessie's pale face, spattered t-shirt and jeans, bleary green eyes. "You okay?"

"Ten hour drive from D.C., mattress the last thing in my rental car."

"My sister Sarah needs to crash here before moving to New York. Sleeping bag on the floor a few days, okay?" Kim's black hair is chin-length, except one gold-tinted, braided strand clipped in a side loop, blue glasses owlish on her tiny nose.

"Sure," Jessie drags the mattress up to her bedroom, unrolls it, sits on the curled edges.

"I'll pick up bread, cheese, chocolate," Kim's out the door.

Jessie's cell phone—Harris.

"Got my visa. No problem writing you into the proposal as you're vetted, experienced." He's holding her note, pretending he's not surprised or upset that she took off.

"I'm in Cambridge, on contract."

"Funding's up in the air, but my friend Krishna's on board. Academia's a shit pile, and what about us?"

Us? Even in bed, no words about feelings.

"No funding, so it's hypothetical?"

"University types will eat your lunch, kick your ass."

"India wasn't exactly gentle on my nerves."

"Snotty bank directors, monkeys on the roof, kid thieves at the Taj Mahal, not a big deal?"

The Taj guide's telling the story of royal love when the woman next to her hisses, "Your bag,"and Jessie yanks her purse strap from a boy's knife. She's grabs for his arm, but he runs.

"Get some sleep, talk tomorrow?" Harris says, not giving up, but feeling his effort fizzle like a sparkler dropped in a puddle.

Jessie puts her phone by the window, missing bossy, opinionated Harris though he laughed when she met an astrologer.

"The stars are speaking? What ridiculous bullshit!" Now he wants her?

The door slams, Kim yelling, "Hungry?"

"My project boss just called, wanting me to dump my job before I start and go to India with him on a grant that may never come through."

"Sounds like love?"

"Word never spoken," Jessie's eyes keep closing.

"Go lie down before you fall over. Tons more to carry upstairs," Kim drops grocery bags in the kitchen, shoves cartons into the living room.

Jessie turns on the fan, flops onto her mattress.

That dream again, in a cycle rickshaw, stalled New Delhi traffic, a woman wearing a faded blue sari is edging between cars and motorbikes, begging, her narrow face marked with sores, hand gesturing toward a sickly-looking baby on her shoulder. Jessie's searching for rupees but a policeman waves the rickshaw forward into a crush of taxis, scooters, bikes, trucks, bullock carts, and the woman's gone, a scrap of paper in the wind. Wakes hearing voices.

Kim's sister, Sarah, is on crutches, elastic bandage wrapping her ankle. Both are Asian, though their mother, Amy, placing a backpack by the window, isn't. Quick smile as she unfolds Sarah's sleeping bag, green with fuchsia flamingos, then heads downstairs for more.

"Babying a sprain," says Sarah, much taller than Kim. "On my way to a ballet intensive in New York. Sorry I woke you clumping up stairs."

"Didn't hear a thing. Dance injury?"

"The truth," says Kim.

"New clogs, twisted my ankle stepping off a curb."

"Ridiculously high clogs."

"You want them, but forget it as they won't fit your big feet," snaps Sarah, swinging her ponytail, showing off her sleek figure in a white t-shirt and black leggings.

"Not my style," laughs Kim, short and square-bodied in jeans, shaking a blue rubber flip-flop at Sarah.

"Need to return my rental." Speedy-Wheels' manager zips through paperwork talking on his cell-phone, never meeting Jessie's eyes.

The bus drops her near an empty storefront with filthy windows, discarded bottles, faded posters next to their three-decker, likely repaired with leftover trim as nothing matches. The small apple tree by the front stairs is dropping rotten fruit, crawling with bees.

Upstairs she finds a sack of potting soil, a clay pot, a dustpan and brush, brought by Kim or her mother. The fern's bruised and wilted, but Jessie plants it, setting it on the window sill near Ganesh.

What about helping impoverished, abused women in India? Somewhere she's got that horoscope, multi-pronged star signs hinting direction, the one Harris considered 'charming nonsense.'

"I'll call him, but need to see Lauren, find Vision International first.

Ganesh is calm, as if everything is as it should be, nothing to worry about. Jessie adjusts her pillow, looks again at the figure balancing on one leg while playing his flute, sleeps.

Paul Perilli

THE TRAIN TO PRAGUE

The train to Prague came to a screeching stop in front of the American couple. Ten minutes later their bags were stored on the overhead rack and they were in window seats facing each other in the second class compartment. Soon after that there was a hiss of compressed air and the train was on its way out of Berlin Hauptbanhhof. Picking up speed, it followed the Spree before turning away from the city.

They shared the compartment with another couple. She had smiled at them and tried to make eye contact as they took their seats by the door, but neither acknowledged her. The man had dark eyes and a day or so growth of whiskers on his cheeks. The woman had brown hair she wore long like someone younger. They were involved in a discussion that had started up the moment they were settled and that seemed urgent. Their voices rose and fell in the small space and sometimes they spoke at the same time. She understood German, but that wasn't the language they were using. She couldn't make out anything and thought they must be Czech. She wasn't sure if they were angry or involved in a topic that required a lot of heavy emphasis. The thought crossed her mind: were they talking about them, the English-speaking vacationers sitting one seat away? Considering the bluster coming out of Washington, much of it directed at America's allies, it didn't seem unreasonable to think that.

She eyed her husband in telepathic inquiry. He gave his shoulders the slightest shrug in reply. His gaze shifted from her to the door as the conductor slid it aside and came into the compartment. He was a tall man wearing a white shirt, an official cap on his head and brown satchel hanging on a shoulder. He checked and punched the tickets of the Czech couple before turning to them.

"I will also need to see your tickets, please," he said.

Her husband slipped the cardstock forms from the jacket and handed them over. The conductor checked and punched them, and when he left the Czech couple went back to their conversation in a way that irritated her. She didn't think it was fair to fill the compartment with only their voices, but she didn't say anything. What would they think of the American couple then? Considering everything going on, why should they yield to another's customs in their own land?

Her husband slept through the stop in Dresden. After it, the train seemed to be in a race with the automobiles on the highway it ran parallel with.

By then the Czech couple were quiet, involved in their own reading. On her iPad she looked over the information about their hotel in Prague. She tapped through the screens of photos and details. It didn't hold her interest. Her thoughts went back to the Czech couple. She wondered how they viewed them, four thousand miles from New York? They weren't supporters of any of it, she had the urge to tell them in their defense. They opposed it. All of it. But the Czech couple stayed focused on their own distractions.

Across the border, there was an announcement in Czech and then English. Over a bridge, the train stopped in an industrial city along a river. There was a change of conductors and they were on the move again, speeding next to a ridge of hills when her husband woke. She handed the plastic container of water to him.

"What did I miss?" he said.

"Nothing much," she said.

"What have you been up to?"

"Checking out the news. Guess who's at it again."

"Oh boy. What is it this time?"

"The caravan. He's not giving up on that. He thinks they're coming to take over the country. He wants his wall."

"What a waste all that is."

"He's never going to let it go."

"I get that." He twisted the cap off the container and took a sip of water. He took another.

"There's no getting away from it," she raised her voice, "not even for a few days over here."

She caught the woman staring at them. Now it was them filling the compartment with their voices.

"It's a bigger mess than I thought it was ever going be, and that's saying a lot," he said.

"I don't see it getting better until..." She cut herself off before she really got going, and that ended the discussion.

The train leaned to the left as it went around a bend. They passed a giant power plant, an indoor market made of sheet metal, and blocks of high-rise housing.

On the other side of a long tunnel they were in the city famous for its Gothic, Renaissance and Baroque buildings and plentiful church spires. The train slowed as it changed tracks and up ahead she saw the platforms of the station. The Czech couple stood and pulled their bags from the overhead rack. They did the same. She put her suitcase on the seat, unzipped the front pocket and slipped the iPad into it. When the train came to a stop the man slid the door aside and turned to them.

"*Hodnì štìstí,*" he said, and nodded, but didn't smile. She looked at the woman.

"He means good luck to you," the woman explained.

"I wish you the same," she said, and smiled.

"Thank you, we will all need it," the woman said, but did not smile back.

The Czech couple stepped into the corridor and they followed behind them, ready to disembark.

Steve Mogg

A VOICE FROM AFAR

'Come to me………..please…………above the shining river, where the great castle once stood……in the lands where the moors and mires look down to the sea. Please come……………please'.

Edlend the Sorcerer awoke with cry. He lay there, covered in perspiration. Rolling off his straw bed he staggered to the window, and looked out at the dense woodland that surrounded his rambling house.

'The dream again', he sighed.

It was the third night running this had happened. He decided he must consult Ancient Glamchek his mentor, and the only other sorcerer in the sprawling Forest of Newn.

As usual, the elderly sorcerer was waiting at the mouth of the crumbling cave that served as his home and place of experimentation.

'I felt you come' said Glamchek 'you are troubled………..an unsolved dream perhaps?'

'Always correct Ancient Friend' answered Edlend 'A dream, thrice dreamed. Always the same message. A woman's voice. Soft and gentle, yet a feeling of fear, desperation perhaps. She calls me, but from where I know not. I have user my scrying skills, but to little affect. She is away to the West, perhaps 3 or 4 days journey by horse, but there is a mist, perhaps some strange force that I am unable to see into.'

For a long hour Glamchek scryed. He too surveyed the impenetrable mist.

'If you wish to know more it seems you must travel to the area. Being closer may make it easier to see the way. I get a feeling of power, and strangely enough………..cunning. Carry all the spells and weapons you can, trust no one. I cannot aid you once you have left the forest.' He opened a cupboard, and pulled a small medallion off the highest shelf. 'This arcane charm may be of some use. Say the words inscribed on the back, and the number of hours you wish. It will then return you, and anything you are wearing or holding, back to the place where you were at that time.'

'Thank you, wise one' said Edlend 'I will travel tomorrow.'

'It is best you go to the city of Xter, which appears to be only a few hours horse-ride from this mist that clouds the mind,' said Glamchek .'Now………… Fare yea well'.

True to his word Edlend rode out the next day, bidding his people to remain loyal and faithful until his return, and putting several additional spells on the house to guard the property. Three uneventful days later he rode into the walled city of Xter. This was the farthest west he had travelled, and he was delighted at the size of the city and the diversity of the people and buildings. Passing a large and well appointed inn he stopped. He looked up at a small window near the roof. For a brief second something touched his mind.

'I believe I should stay here tonight' he thought. After seeing his horse was well looked after, he put on his Sorcerer's Cloak, and strode into the hostelry. The Innkeeper noticed him straight away and gave him food, drink and the finest room.

'He appears to regard me with some awe, perhaps sorcerers have a bad reputation here' thought Edlend. He was still thinking of the fine meal when the Innkeeper came over to him and bowed.

'Master' said the Innkeeper with due deference 'I would ask a favour of you, of which I am prepared to pay whatever you ask. But, before I ask this favour, I have a special beverage called Kawfee not seen in these parts for generations.'

The Innkeeper offered up a large earthenware mug, full to the brim with a dark brown steaming liquid. Edlend thanked him, and passed unknown to the Innkeeper, a small talisman over it. This checked for poisons it might harbour. Deciding it was safe to drink Edlend slowly drank it down.

'Well ! Master Innkeeper' said Edlend, 'That was very good, a little bitter, but enjoyable, thank you. Now, I believe you need a favour.'

'Lord' replied the Innkeeper 'I know you to be a Sorcerer by your cloak and the items you carry with you'.

'True' replied Edlend, 'but surely you have other people of my calling in so large a city'.

'Once, perhaps Sire, but not for many years now.'

'Strange' said Edlend, 'no matter. Your request good landlord.'

The Innkeeper sat opposite Edlend.

'It is my young daughter. A few days ago she became unwell. My wife feeds and looks after her, but all day she sits in a chair looking out of the window. She says nothing and does not know me, her eyes glazed. Yesterday I consulted a local wise woman who suggested that my daughter was in a trance and only sorcery could help. I was at my wits end, then I saw you arrive, and realised it was no mere chance that you came here.'

'Tis true' said Edlend 'I am answering a summons, but not from your daughter. Nevertheless, take me to her, and I will see if there is anything that can be done'.

Two women watched over the girl, but left when Edlend and the Innkeeper entered. Edlend made several magic passes over her and chanted a short spell.

'She is bewitched' he said.

'Ah...........what can be done.......this is terrible.........why her?' ranted the Innkeeper

'Quiet!' shouted Edlend 'Something happens'.

In his mind he heard the woman's voice again, calmer and softer.

'You are closer...........I can tell............have you found the child?'

'Yes' thought Edlend, forcing his thoughts towards the young girl. 'I stand by the girl'

'I will talk through her...............it will be easier to form my thoughts'

The little girl coughed and cleared her throat, and turned towards Edlend. Watching her carefully he cast the runes of the '3 truthful answers'. It was unlikely that anyone would tell a lie without twitching or fidgeting when under such a powerful spell.

'Hello' said the little girl 'I am called Lucia. I am Princess and Sorceress of The Tawbayee. My people live by the sea, a day's journey from the old city of Xter.'

'Do you know where you are?' questioned Edlend.

'I have been imprisoned for at least ten days. I only have the description I told you about when you heard my dream-call. For several days my mind was confused, and I felt dazed. I am back to normal now and realise I have been captured by someone with greater powers than myself. A mind-mist surrounds me so I cannot see outside my room, though I believe I am underground.' answered the Innkeepers daughter.

'How did you know about the shining river with its great castle?' questioned Edlend again.

'It was in my mind when I awoke, though it means nothing to me.' She replied.

'Can you tell me anymore things that may help me in finding you?' questioned Edlend for the third time.

'My room is very large and smells sweet like a spring meadow. It has white marble floors and walls, like only the finest palaces are said to have. There is a large comfortable bed, chairs and a finely carved wooden table. There is only one large oak door and no windows. I am given three excellent meals every day, served by strange people with green tinted skin. They appear to be bewitched. Fresh clothes are bought to me each day. I seem to have everything I want except my freedom.' The girl stopped for a moment then said 'Will you come?'

'Yes,' replied Edlend 'I will try to reach you again when I am closer. Meanwhile, release the child.'

The child sneezed three times and turned to the innkeeper. 'Hello Father, I dreamt I was in a great palace with strange people......... I am awfully hungry.'

'Thank you, thank you' said the Innkeeper joyfully.

'Innkeeper,' said Edlend 'a favour from you'.

'Anything. Anything' answered the Innkeeper eagerly.

'I need a guide who knows the hills and moorlands well'.

'Ah! There is a man staying at the Inn today. He comes here occasionally. A traveller of some sort. A quiet and thoughtful man who pays me well and purports to know the moorlands. I will talk to him straight away.'

With that the Innkeeper took the hand of his daughter and hurried from the room.

Tomorrow came, and Edlend surveyed his guide. The Innkeeper had insisted on paying for the guides' services, and had refused all payment for the Sorcerers' stay. Before bidding farewell the Innkeeper gave Edlend a package.

'This is the beverage you drank yesterday. I have ground the beans into a fine powder and packed it carefully less the taste dissipates. I believe it should make twenty mugful's'.

The guide talked little, but had a friendly aura, so Edlend followed him into the foothills. It was approaching midday when the guide reined in his horse.

'See that stream?' he said

Edlend looked up at saw a narrow waterfall cascading over a cliff barely a hundred paces away from them.

'I think this is the one you are looking for. We must wait to be sure'

A few minutes went by, suddenly the sun shone through the overcast sky. The colour of the stream changed from a cold dull grey to a brilliant silver, reflecting minerals in the surrounding rocks. Edlend noticed that the cliff tops had an artificial look, as if in the distant past they had been carved, or perhaps placed there deliberately.

'The Shining River, the Great Castle, the Moorlands' mused Edlend. 'This is indeed the place I seek' he turned to speak, but the guide had vanished.

'Well! No matter', thought Edlend 'I can see a pathway to the summit'.

In the distance to the East he could make out a smoke haze from the chimneys of Xter. To the South a line of blue where the sea began. To the North and West hills and moorland. Suddenly he heard raised voices. Dismounting he removed his cloak, and packed it into his saddlebags. Underneath he wore a chain-mail vest and the leather and metal clothing usually associated with a mercenary. He attached Glamchek's medallion to his wrist bracelet. He read and memorised the short rune on the back. Then with the aid of the 'Spell of Sameness' melted into his surroundings. Throwing the saddlebags over his shoulder he crept past a line of rocks until he saw the origin of the voices.

Three men, one a merchant by his hat and bright clothing, were unloading supplies from a horse-drawn cart. They were outside a high wooden doorway that was set into the rock-face. Several green tinted people were collecting the goods and taking them through the doorway.

'Hurry' shouted the merchant 'The sooner I leave this blighted place the better' He turned to one of the green people 'Do you have my gold? I would be on my way. I'll not travel on these moor-lands after nightfall.'

Without saying a word the green man threw a small bag to the merchant. The merchant looked inside and nodded 'I suppose that'll do' he said grumpily.

Edlend cast 'The short spell of Invisibility'. He then stepped out from behind the rocks and walked briskly towards the door. The merchant whipped the horses and the cart moved off. The green people picked up the last of the boxes and Edlend squeezed between them and entered the passageway behind the doorway. Following the green people he eventually came to a large ill lit storeroom. Off to the right was a kitchen area, and once through that he came to a wide passage with several large wooden doors.

The spell wore off and he could be seen again. Hurriedly, he walked down the passageway. At each doorway he stopped and threw a non-formed thought a short distance. At the third doorway it bounced off Lucia.

'You are here'

'Outside your door' thought Edlend, and turned the handle. To his surprise the door opened, and he stepped into the room. Lucia stood by a large oak table sipping a glass of wine.

'Hello' she said 'Thank you for coming to my aid so quickly. How did you open the door, it has always been secured with all manner of spells, locks and guards?'

Edlend walked over to her. She was younger than him, though older than he had expected, perhaps thirty years of age.

'Good morrow Princess Lucia' he bowed slightly 'getting in was far too easy. Leaving may prove to be harder.'

'True', a voice from behind him boomed out. 'For indeed I have you both now'

Edlend turned. It was the guide from the Inn, but now dressed in an elaborate Sorcerer's cloak, and carrying a tall wooden staff topped with a glowing red crystal.

'Why all this intrigue?' said Edlend 'If you wanted to see me I would have come'.

'Perhaps' said the Sorcerer.

'Perhaps' replied Edlend. 'Still, I am here now, and the Princess is your prisoner, so what do you want of me?'

'Nothing' said the Sorcerer.

'Strange to come so far for nothing?' queried Edlend.

'You, the Princess and the ancient one are the only Sorcerers left within five days ride of this place. The ancient one will no longer leave the forest, therefore you two are the only threat to my future ambitions....'.

'How do you feel we pose a threat?' interrupted Edlend.

'I intend to have supreme rule over Xter, the moors, and lands around in the weeks to come. I will extend this area in the coming years. When this starts to happen people will come to you and beg for your help to oppose me. I cannot allow this.' The Sorcerer paused and in a quieter tone continued 'I considered having you killed, but your talents may be of use to me, therefore I will keep you here in this place until that time. You should have everything you need.....'

'Except our freedom,' said Lucia.

The Sorcerer just laughed.

Edlend considered making a move towards the Sorcerer then noticed a slight shimmer around him.

'A projection' he thought 'the best I've ever seen'.

The Sorcerer was outside the room, and could be anywhere in the castle, so there was little he could do.

'Well you have us, and there is nothing we can achieve by opposing your wishes' he said to the projection and looking around continued 'You are right. We are well accommodated. Is boiling water available?'

'A strange request,' said the Sorcerer 'there are spells available, nevertheless, I will have a container sent to you.' So saying he vanished.

'A clever projection' said Edlend, and turning to Lucia removed a package from his saddlebags.

The door opened and a green tinted man carried in a small metal pot. He left without saying a word, and as with the previous encounter Edlend noticed the glazed eyes and slow deliberate walk of a person under enchantment. Taking out two earthenware mugs and using some fine material as a filter, placed some of the Kawfee onto the filter.

Lucia watched him intently whilst he poured the boiling water over it.

'I've not seen this magic before' she commented.

'Not magic. I am thirsty after my ride and I thought a hot drink suitable before we leave,' replied Edlend.

He handed her a mug, and then to show her it was safe, immediately started to sip the beverage from the other mug. After a minute or so she started to drink.

'It's a little bitter' she said 'perhaps some herbs or even a little milk mixed in would help.'

'Yes. A good idea' he replied. 'We will try this next time'

'I'll mention this to the green servants,' she said.

'No need for that' said Edlend 'We won't be here that long. Finish your drink and gather your belongings and we will go.'

'I have none,' said Lucia. 'Even the gown I wear was given to me'.

'Hold my hand,' said Edlend.

He then touched his wrist bracelet against his forehead and muttered the spell. Finally he thought of the number 24.

The room slowly faded until they were surrounded by a purple mist. There was a sudden flash and they were sitting at a wooden bench.

'Master' said a familiar voice 'My apologies, I did not see you return. How careless of my servants not to tell me. A lady too..........would you care to eat now or later.'

'This' said Edlend to Lucia 'is my good friend the Innkeeper. This must be lunchtime and this the dining area of the Inn where I was sitting exactly one day ago, and yes we will eat now, and when we have finished a mug each of that splendid Kawfee. Oh! And this time perhaps some honey to mellow the taste'.

'Do you think the Sorcerer will follow us?' questioned Lucia

'I'm sure he will' replied Edlend 'but not for some days. So until he does let's eat, drink and make merry.'

In the ruined castle on the moors the Sorcerer gazed at a large crystal and sighed.

Steve Morris

READ FACE

"You're telling me there's an App come out for phones that tells you whenever anyone is lying to you? No way!"

I shook my head in disbelief when listening to my friend's news at the end of the week. He usually called around on Friday nights as he went to a different college than me. His life *always* seemed more eventful than mine and he was always the first to know what was going on.

"How can you *not* have heard about it?" he asked, also shaking his head. "*Read Face,* it's called. It's true. You just focus your phone's camera on someone's face and this App analyses scientifically *the way* that they're talking. Then through your earphones it tells you whether they are telling the truth or lying to you. Some teenagers came up with the idea."

"Oh I see. Works like a lie detector, then?" I suggested. "A sort of polygraph."

"Way more than that. This one listens and learns. First you get it to focus on someone for a while. It works best if they don't know you're doing it, then they're behaving naturally. The App works by analysing their eye movements and facial expressions alongside the words they're coming out with when they talk. For the first hour or so all you might get is *Lie* or *Truth* through your earphones every now and again but then after some time it begins to catch up with what is being said."

To be fair, this was getting interesting.

He went on.

"All you need is a phone with a half decent camera. The trouble is that the App is still really expensive to download at the moment. No wonder it's mainly been celebrities who have been playing about with it. They always get everything first, eh?"

I nodded.

"Does it *really* work, though?" I asked.

"Work?" he repeated. "It's deadly accurate. Someone 'borrowed' their father's phone with the App in college on Wednesday. Everyone was testing it out in class on one another all morning. You'd be amazed the things they found out! I'm telling you, there were red faces all day. Another feature of the App is it gives every target subject a 'percentage truth' score. That works out the ratio of how much truth someone tells out of all the things they say."

This didn't quite add up to me. I had to ask some more.

"But what if your phone camera can't get a clear view of the target subject, say if they are sitting right behind you?" I asked. "And anyway many people like me for example don't like having a smartphone camera pointing at them and I certainly watch what I'm saying if I know I'm being recorded! I think most people do, to be fair."

"Well, there's a premium version coming out too. Not just telling you 'truth' or 'lie'. If the phone mic can pick their voice up clearly for long enough, then eventually based on sound signals in their speech alone it begins to tell you if they are telling the truth or not. And if you can get just a few minutes view of their face while they are talking it begins to translate what they are *really* thinking onto your phone screen while they are jabbering away. Uses a 'more advanced algorithm' whatever that means. Not cheap, by all accounts," my friend informed me.

"Where does he pick up this stuff every week?" I wondered as always.

We missed meeting the next week but exactly a fortnight later we met up again. It was another Friday night and he had come around to my place as usual. However, a lot had happened in the meantime and neither of us had a particularly fun couple of weeks. Interestingly however, it seemed that nobody else had either.

At least two couples in my street had split up in the preceding days. One neighbour had been sacked from their job. I'd noticed only that very day that a number of people in the town centre were walking around sporting black eyes or were on crutches. Other people were literally not speaking to one another. There had been a spate of car vandalism on our estate. Police sirens were heard most of the day and night without a break. Tabloids were publishing league tables of politicians based on Read Face's *Percentage Truth*. Most concerning of all, was that the murder rate nationally was on the rise.

"No. It seems that things are not good anywhere at the moment," we agreed.

As usual, and it being the end of two weeks since we last met up, my friend recounted the packed fortnight he'd just had.

"This is all since *Read Face* came out. Did I tell you my brother was turned down flat for both car insurance *and* for health insurance this week? My boss from my evening job had a letter from his life insurance company saying they've gone and cancelled his policy and won't be refunding his premium because he had *lied.* I'm keeping well out of his way. He was already wound up enough after his wife booted him out of their house. Guess why!"

"Oh I can guess. That's not good," I replied.

"And it gets worse. The college year is nearly over as you know. Have you tried applying for any jobs at the moment?" he asked. "You're fine until you get to the interview! Then they're obviously recording you with *Read Face*. The thing is, you'd think there would be loads of job vacancies available because everyone else is getting fired at the moment!"

I added, "Have you also noticed that the President has stopped doing any interviews? Not even on the radio. He's still wearing a mask in public. Have you seen that? In fact, everyone on the TV seems to be wearing a face mask again even though the scientists said we were clear of the Pandemic five years ago!"

"Tell me about it. You've seen the news headlines on TV tonight? Punch ups. Divorces, Fights. They're blaming *Read Face*," my friend pointed out.

"Anyway, I've heard it's already starting to get banned in some countries," I added. "The service providers there are sending out an update which deletes it from your phone. We'll be next. It is only a matter of time before the same thing happens here. Perhaps they need to do before the whole country closes down!"

"Hey. Do you want a go? Before they delete it?" my friend suddenly asked out of the blue.

"You've got it on your phone?"

"Oh yes. Had to try it," he answered, showing me the instantly recognisable blue screen of *Read Face.*

"And you've been recording me?" I assumed.

"Of course I have. Er, no mate. You'd have noticed!" my friend assured me, caught slightly off guard for once. I was convinced he *had* been using the App on me.

All that evening we tried it out on each other. Try as we might, we couldn't catch it out. We couldn't kid it and get a lie past it. However, as we valued our friendship we were both careful in the questions we asked each other so as not to trigger that certain word to appear on the phone screen that would have caused an irreparable argument. We'd seen what it had done to people.

We had to admit that the software certainly seemed to work on us. Pointing the phone at people on the TV didn't do the trick, however. Interestingly TV presenters must have been aware of this as they hadn't resorted to wearing face masks again. They knew that for the time being at least they were safe from being caught out by the *Read Face* App.

Scarves had come back into fashion along with large sunglasses and baseball hats. Politicians turned up their coat collars. An online ad sold cosmetic surgery that could protect you from this type of 'facial dialogue translation software.'

It had made the news again that night.

"Why is it getting banned, though?" I asked "Just because it helps us find out when we're not hearing the truth. Why is that so wrong?"

A government Minister went as far as making an official statement the next day:

We have become aware of a new smartphone app called Read Face. While there is <u>no</u> scientific evidence that Read Face works and that the output is fictitious and based on a random algorithm, it must be remembered that the app was designed for entertainment purposes only. However, we are concerned that the app could be misused to cause distress amongst unaware members of the public and therefore we are today asking all service providers to disable access to Read Face with immediate effect.

The original developers also issued a statement that it was not meant to be used for anything other than fun. So there it was. *Read Face* had been discredited. It was an unusual step for a government to intervene in this way but people had taken it seriously and had misused it. During the following week updates were sent out to all devices. These effectively removed the App from everyone's phones. Despite the best efforts of many, no one could get it to work from then on.

Inevitably in the ever faster world we live in, people moved on. *Read Face* became yesterday's news.

About a year later my friend was (wrongly) arrested by the police due to being in the wrong place at the wrong time in connection with a rather unpleasant motoring offence. He was interrogated for some time but released later the same day after the real culprit was caught. The day being Friday, he ended up around my house telling me all about it. For once I didn't envy his experiences!

"They kept asking the same questions," he said. "And I kept giving the same answers, even when they were trying to catch me out. The accident happened right in front of me. I saw it all but they weren't happy with my statement and they seemed convinced that I was making it all up. After some time I noticed that one of the police officers was pointing a smartphone toward me. I managed to catch a glimpse of the reflection of the screen in his glasses…

"Anyway they charged the real suspect in the end. At least it's all over and they let you go free," I shrugged, offering him a drink.

…The police detectives knew I was telling the truth all along because they were using the *Read Face* app," he said.

SHORT ESSAY

Lenora Rain-Lee Good

NECESSARY FAREWELLS

A farewell is necessary before you can meet again. ~Richard Bach

Birthdays and aging were the topics of conversation one day when I mentioned I stopped having birthdays. Auntie informed me that, "she who has the most birthdays, lives longest." She collected more than 90 before she stopped.

What Auntie never told me was that she who lives longest also says the most 'goodbyes'.

Lieutenant Graham, USWAC, loved her fiancé, a Green Beret stationed in 'Nam. When he was killed, she said her goodbye, and with her Army-issued .45, chose her 'cide. My goodbye was written on my tears.

Bud loved his wife of 30 good years. Two years after Babe's death, Bud drove down a lonely road, stopped his truck, got out, sat on a big rock, smoked some cigarettes, then joined her. My goodbyes found them when I burned the letters I wrote and the smoke carried them to heaven.

Too many of my loved ones died on different Christmas Days. For me, Christmas is a day of death, a Day of Mourning. I spend it alone with beloved ghosts.

Steve loved life. He fought to keep it 8 years after his diagnosis. Finally, he could fight no more. His beloved wife, my good friend, called me. I got to tell him I loved him, and would support his decision, and would be there for his wife. I didn't want him to do it, but I understood. My friend took a long walk and came home a widow.

I dreamed a dead friend into being, just for a while, back in my life. He, his wife, some other friends, and I were on a public bus going into town to see a live performance of Tilting at Windmills by Don Quixote. We were all on the bus, laughing and joking, and talking about how appropriate that Steve would come back to visit for that play. As he stepped off the bus, he smiled and wondered aloud if Don Quixote would be there, too?

I woke with a smile, at having seen my friend, and how happy he was, and how healthy. I woke before the play began, so don't know if the author appeared or not. It doesn't matter. What matters was seeing and being with my friend, Steve, for the short time allowed. Hearing his laugh, seeing his smile, seeing how much he still loves Philippa.

I am now old enough that many of the goodbyes I say are to those much younger. Saying goodbye is not as hard as it used to be, especially now that I can dream my friends and family into visits, short though they may be.

I intend to collect many more birthdays.

USWAC-United States Women's Army Corps. The WAC has long since been absorbed into the US Army.

Alan Elyshevitz

NAMING THE WILDFIRE

The big ice is gone, the big rain, too, leaving
us with a posthumous sky: sorties of embers
and contrails of suppressant. Bird life scoured
from enfeebled trees, the red-hot tingle of shifting
wind repels men wearing bright retardant.
In a sump of the forest, fish life turns insoluble
in a parboiled pond. The one road out disintegrates.
Fuel trucks hug their sides. No household picnic
can withstand assault on paper plates and
Adirondack chairs when the conflagration
hungers for refreshment. Let's call this one
the Wedding Cake Fire, measure its acreage
hour by hour, honeymoon at a makeshift
encampment with a view of permanent sundown.

Alessio Zanelli

THE ARROW OF TIME

Her lineaments remind me of an angel,
although I've never seen one,
unless in some past life
I subconsciously remember.
I often find myself wondering about it.
Visions, déjà vu and premonitions,
do all such things make sense?
They say the arrow cannot be reversed,
that's an unquestionable law of physics,
a hard, undesirable rule of reality,
but it's only valid for matter and energy,
whereas remembrance is made of neither.
Maybe memories move through time,
I think they really do, both ways.
So, the angel I seem to recognize in her face
may be one I'll see in the future
or even in some other life to come,
whose recollection travels backwards in time.
That's how the arrow can be actually reversed.
That's how humangelical features hold me in doubt.

Amanda Blue Leigh

THE SEED SOWER

*AMANDABLEIGH.7..2020

She finds the seeds
Underground
Where no one would look
Unless they knew
Not where you might think
Underneath the skin
Corridors filled with images
Flying wild into sensations
Words given
Out of thin air
Offerings
Dreams
Visions
Tools to believe in
Some
Thing
Making mystical stories out of our lives
Seeds of secrets
Seeds of healing
Seeds of knowledge
Seeds of sound
Seeds of feeling
Seeds of worth
She carries them close
They blow away freely
Sewn into the collective field
It is no longer between us

Our field belongs to One giant world
Veins of bloodlines
Light and Truth
Thinking, living, breathing
Her
Who knows how many?
Who knows, so many unnamed ...?
Does it really matter ?
When every part of her is in the seed
Every part is saved
She has become completely herself
She Is the Seed Sower

*@]`,~~~~~~~ AB

David Flynn

THE PERIOD

You have claws.
Your blue eyes grow black, your wide eyes narrow.
That howling that comes from the bedroom
is you, calling other women.
Your body glows red.
A trickle of blood
runs down your nose.
"I hate you. You are
the root-cause of all disease,"
and your bell of voice
scrapes and clangs, whines.

I keep to my office,
with the moose head on the wall.
For a few days we will fire rockets
in the war between male and female.
Then you will come home.

Dion O'Reilly

WADING

In these days of disease, I am visited
by two friends. We dress in our ugliest
Tevas, straw hats and shorts, to escape—

like I escaped as a kid—
through forget-me-nots, poison oak,
patches of light and periwinkle—
to the creek— vale of my childhood, nearly unreachable,
water-carved furrow to the sea.

Can air smell like sorrow? I've lived here
all my life. No, this creek has kept me here,
like a blanket a baby can't give up.

It opens me, the way each bend opens
to a new pocket of air,
another clutch of pollywogs,
beady crawdads, a kind of tufted duck.

When I wend around a certain turn,
I know I'll see Kev's ghost slumming
at the swim hole, where we dove off cliffs,
like lords of air, into cool water.

He's still fourteen, smoking in a surplus jacket,
rubbing ashes on his jeans.
He still bears the silence of the fatherless,

never mentions why his mother left him
to live with Gran'ma Muster in a motorhome.
And I, too, kept my mother's secrets,
the way she rewrote my life

with her loops of cursive
inscribed on back and thighs,
whip flicked like a tamer's.

If Kev's alive, why doesn't he wade with me?
Like I thought we would forever,
listening to the water's answers
to problems we couldn't name.

Don Schaeffer

CITIZENSHIP INTERVIEW

And what is your address?

.

Exactly? I am in an I.
A bubble in a time that has
no number. You understand.

.

Yes.

.

I am in creaturehood,
realm of the possible,
wrapped in flesh with an outside and an in.

.

I'm writing this down.

.

I am in the needing of light
with ups and downs
stretched in myself
and the state of flowing.

.

Yes, I noticed. You have that accent.

.

Well there is a planet
do you have a name for it on your grid?
It's not heaven.

.

Yes. And what is your state of size.

.

I am in the state of weight-fulness
solidity, not floating.

Multi-moleculed and a hollow city.
I am large enough to stay anchored.
I cling to an orbit. I'm in motion
all the time, around an X, Y, Z, but that is all.
I'm in the state of you and me
mostly not alone. A structured memory
and a district of models and designs.

.

Oh that kind!

.

If you want, I can provide the numbers and names.

.

Not necessary. That's just a detail.

.

I am in a classified district and a body in a building in a room
and laying in a bed that was granted me. I barley know how.

.

Ok. I can find you.

Emiliana Russo

LAERTES[1]

everyone stays
in this castle,
at the court of king claudius.

everyone lives
to serve,
to be a subject.

but I do not.

I do not belong to
this castle, to
this court, to
the asphyctic denmark.

I was not born to die in
this fortress, secluded
from the world, without
virtute and *canoscenza.*[2]

I must leave.
I will never come back,
never.

---

[1] Laertes is one of the characters in *Hamlet* by Shakespeare.

[2] Quoting Ulysses in *The Divine Comedy* by Dante Alighieri: "[…] fatti non foste a viver come bruti,/ ma per seguir virtute e canoscenza." ("you were not made to live like brutes, but to follow **virtue** and **knowledge**", emphasis is mine)." Dante Alighieri et al. *The Divine Comedy of Dante Alighieri. Volume 1, Inferno.* New York: Oxford University Press, 1996, pp. 404-405.

Eric tessier

ERIK SATIE, THE MARATHON RUNNER AND THE PIANIST

He was both an artist and the greatest athlete in his category
The word "athlete" must rather sound funny when speaking of Erik Satie
Indeed Satie has nothing to do with a bodybuilder
He was not physically very impressive, in his velvet suit and tie
His small pince-nez high above the bridge of his nose, his umbrella
And his bowler hat.

He really does look like a clerk or an underpaid teacher
Nevertheless he was one of the most talented composers of his generation
Debussy loved his music, and has orchestrated a few of his works
For Satie was mostly a piano player–even though he can write for an orchestra
But he struggled with determination to earn his living with the help of his beloved keyboard
Rarely in prestigious venues.

Actually he played all night long in the bars and cabarets of Montmartre
Between dances and cancan, the shrieks of the whores and the growls of the Apaches
As the bad boys were called at the time; between the heavy smoke of cigars and cigarettes
The glass of wine, beer and absinthe; between the insults, the cheating card-players
He kept hammering the keys, playing popular songs so that everyone could sing along
His feet beating time.

Erik Satie was an extremely poor but an extremely proud person
Nobody would have guessed how poverty-stricken he was.
And he wouldn't have told anybody even though he was sometimes
about to faint
In the wee hours, after the patrons had left or slept head on the table
Too drunk to go home, he often refused a cab, proclaiming he'd rather
walk a while
To breathe some fresh air.

The truth was he couldn't afford a cab; his earnings were low and he
wanted to keep them
To buy food. So he walked home alone the twenty-one kilometers
between Montmartre
And his place, in Arcueil, a small city in the Val-de-Marne district.
Exhausted by a night's work, he did it nonetheless everyday of the week
His fingers and feet hurt, he felt foggy-minded, sometimes on the verge
of falling asleep
While walking. He crossed path with early workers, policemen waiting
for their nightshift to finish

The marathon runner–or walker–took the place of the piano player
And traveled the long deserted streets of Paris, before entering the suburb
Funny as it looks, Satie then was a real athlete, far more resistant than the thugs
Who used to yell at him: "Play another one, pal, are you tired already?"
The most difficult was probably to climb the stairs leading to his one-
room apartment
Located on the last storey of the house.

Unfortunately for the sport, Erik Satie continued to compose music
Did he miss a career? Did we miss a champion? We'll never know
But music lovers don't care at all–who would blame them? It isn't
because they despise sport
But listen to Les Gymnopédies or Les Gnossienes and you'll understand why.
As for Satie, he sure smiles at the idea. At last, he's resting now, in the
cemetery of Arcueil.

Gary Beck

HAZARDOUS DUTY

First responders
are mostly forgotten
except in a crisis,
the moment of need
when against all logic
they bravely rush
into threats of death
to rescue strangers,
who suddenly appreciate
the dangers faced
in recurring hazards.

NO STORM WARNING

Harmony is interrupted
by surprise detonations
of emotional outrage
at the real, imagined,
offenses suddenly viral
infecting those exposed
to unexpected fury,
difficult to sooth.

George K. Karos

THE SIGHTLESSNESS OF GOD

God is everywhere no one can see.
Time expands our lucid dreams
As progress yields what neither known nor been
Feeding fears' oil to fuel freedoms engine
over bridges navigated through rough terrain
to transport our needs and planned intentions
proclaiming our worth and craved destinations
safely guiding us all now or then again
to empathy shared by sisterhood and man.

WE ARE TAKING A VOTE

Our families, mine and yours,
Will soon be taking a vote
To confirm our joint existences.
We are seeking proof of both
Past and present futures
Through the act of an election
That will select further leaderships
For us and our anonymously sanctioned.

Gordana Radovanović

PERHAPS YOU'RE SLEEPING

Perhaps you're sleeping in the arms of fog,
or on the pillow of purple shadows.
While here, they're pouring dusk with the scent of soil,
and Gypsies nomads are bivouacking,
and some girl is coming down the garden,
accompanied by marigolds' song
and fern fondling.

Perhaps you're dreaming in some olive-wood,
with a rosemary branch in clenched fist.
While here, night's threatening my memory,
and lindens are blooming in eyes,
and melancholy is, like a smoke,
stealing away under the threshold,
slowly thickening and aching.

Perhaps you're smiling while the dream's taking you
along the sandy coast towards the light.
But you know that there's really gloom everywhere,
and that night can't be shackled,
the last star has to fall down,
flowers to crumble,
and the pain to pass by.

Perhaps you don't and you didn't exist.
Perhaps you're a vision even in my memory.
But I still believe your eyes
and every day, I see the sun off to the edge of the forest
and leave the quenched fires behind me.

Perhaps you're sleeping,
while the fogs are rising,
and I'm still telling you the same poem.

Translation from the original Serbian language into English was made by the author Gordana Radovanović.

Greg Farnum

JUSTICE

It must have happened
Somewhere

Someone

MUST HAVE

RESISTED ARREST
BEFORE

they got
beaten, tased
shot...

KaZ Akers

LET GO OF YOUR HATE

Don't let the haters
make you a hater.
Hating haters is just as hateful
as haters hating.
Hate today and you will hate tomorrow.
Haters hate movers and shakers
so move it and shake it
and leave the hating to the haters.
When you start hating
hating is hard to stop.
You may end up hating yourself for hating.
(You see where I'm going?)
Hate does not stop with hate
it starts with hate.
In the end
it's not hating your hate
that lets go of your hate.
It's loving the hate our of your hate
that lets go of your hate.

Keith Moul

QUERIES REGARDING TIME AND MEN

Light surrounds voluptuous swaying maples.
Not much time left. This light is here, offers
no rising smokestack to a star or another kind
of magnificence. I move to it, drawn strongly
toward the dusk, encroaching. Light is gone.

A crackling place of fallen and falling leaves
meets me at the new edge of dark, leaves soon
to decompose. Bereft but not beggarly, think
of them as leavings to good time, anchorage
in the wake of time. I come here alone, to be
in a sense timeless, no need of root, no need
of light, becalmed in harbor, moored securely.

Spread about are cottonwoods, already snowing;
firs ready to burst; and alders inclined to shriek,
but standing still, in respect if not also rectitude.

In contrast, loud young men arrive in the forest.
I am much older, of course; I do not discourage
fun, but am I less the man to prefer my solitude?
or seek able young allies to authenticate a future?

LC Gutierrez

JEKYLL SHOULD HAVE KNOWN

he could have concentrated
and syringed the stuff
straight into the vein,
a hot rush.

Or crystallized and chopped up cold,
like powdered snow,
might avoid the pallid razored image,
a face half his own,
through a rolled up receipt
from the apothecary
blown it fast up his nose.

Or off the back-bar,
from a bottle racked up straight,
next to another hard and dark
and full of absinthe,
like twin sarcophagi,
would've surely seeped through
his thick Mr. Hyde.

Not thinking clearly,
but he had all the tools.

Yet sharp enough to quit
the shell game.
The chemical roulette,
The behind which door.
The open up and step off
into the self-same hole.
The fix that just don't fix.

Lenora Rain-Lee Good

WHAT MAKES A LAND HOLY?

What makes a land holy?
Is it the people who lived on
and loved it, who died
protecting it, their families,
their loved ones buried there?

> *How would your heart change if I told you Jesus Christ had*
> *already come back for the second time and got crucified again?*
> *He called himself Crazy Horse and never said anything about a*
> *third attempt.*
> —Sherman Alexie, Year of the Indian

Is it the people who still live there,
who care for the land, who respect
the land of their birth,
the land of their mothers,
the land of their elders?

> A brother and sister were playing with toys / when their room exploded. //
> *In what language / is this holy?*
> —Naomi Shihab Nye, All Things Not Considered.

Perhaps it is the mythology
that one or more of their gods
was born there, died there,
resurrected there,
and never saw a reason to leave?

> *His mouth full / of broken syllables, / Mario dies a death / with*
> *each twisted word / he utters*
> —Lynn M. Knapp, Crossing

Maybe that the Grandfathers and Grandmothers
carved it, stacked it, furrowed it,
colored it with white and brown, purple and green,
[no new stanza]

red and yellow—painted the lands
their favorite colors?

   Thanks for the tree / between me & a sniper's bullet.
     —Yusef Komunyakaa, Thanks

What makes a land holy?
I don't know—but I know
when I stand on it and the world goes hush
and I hear the holy song, think the holy thoughts,
and know the love of all my relations.

   When asked what happens at the moment of death,
   Raven sat silently, then said, "I give away my belongings."
     —Robert Aitken, Death

Mark Tulin

SCARECROW

I see you staring at me,
not the most handsome
with your wooden arms,
all full of straw
in an Iowa cornfield
as if you were impersonating
a hillbilly farmer
made of flesh and bones

You don't frighten me
in your flannel shirt
and dirty overalls
I wasn't a crow born yesterday
I'm not going to fall for your
human schemes and tricks
You're not going to chase me
from your delicious crops and seeds.

Michael H. Brownstein

AFTERWARDS

We awake to a place we do not understand
folds of skin starch empty of breath.
The nearby stream the only space it knows,
the river trapped in the channel it creates for itself.
and boulder puddles eroding into muddy flesh.
Dragons seek nourishment in the clouds
and the vapor streams we toss around
feed the other animals hiding in the sky.
Everywhere a bounty of molecules
stretches hands across itself
and we who come to this place far from memory
breath an air full of nourishment and satisfaction.

THIS IS NOT REALLY WHO ANY OF US ARE

a contour of disfigurement
and the small rash of dust
within recession and depression--

keep this skin folded,
let your breath recoil,
remember always,

here in the Valley of Large Prints,
the Layer of Cave and Dwelling,
a place called You Are Loved exists

Prof. Moshé Liba

EARTH OF FIRE

to Natanel Lorch

Burns the bush
in the desert
Burns the village
in Russia
Burns the Auto-da-Fé
In Spain, in Portugal
Burns the Inquisition
In the New World
Burn Melaj, Hara
in Tunis, in Djerba, in Meknes
Burns the village
by the Cossacks in Ukraine
Burn the cremation ovens
in Auschwitz, Majdanek
Burn the mass graves
of Babi-Yar, Treblinka
Burn the Jewish tents
at the Berlin Crystal Night
Burns the Ghetto
in Warsaw
Burns the Masada fortress
on the shores of the Dead Sea
Burns the Temple of Jerusalem
the First, the Second
Burns the Hill
of the Third
Burn the fox tails
in the Philistine fields

Burn tire rubbers in the streets
of Gaza, Samaria, Judea
Burn the trees
in the woods of Keren Kayemet
Burn the chicken coops
on Moshav Mountain
Burn the borders
in the north, east and south
Burns the Golden Calf
in the Sinai Desert
Burns the Pillar of Fire
showing the people their way
Burn the Holy Books
the Bible rolls, the Tables of the Law
Burns the bush, the Ghetto,
the tents, the ovens, the temple
They burn, in each generation,
thousand years without a break
What a burning life
that of the Chosen People!

ENEMY BROTHER

The baby
hyena
kills its newborn
brother
to reserve for itself
the breast milk.
The mother,
does not intervene.
There is not
father
in the cave.
Cain
killed his brother

to reserve for himself
the divine favors.
There was not
mother
and the father
of the earth
did not intervene.

NEITHER SMOKE, NOR PERFUME

Don't smoke
the cigarette smells like fire
the village burns, Guevalt!
and odor of the corpses
burning in the Valley of the killings,
smell of blood
and rotten meat
in the mass graves.
The smoke brings me continuously
odor of the crematory ovens
that chased away even
the prey birds.

And please don't sprinkle
essences on me,
is the scent of perfume
that the Nazis used
to escape the stench
and to wash their hands
with Jewish lard soap.

And asking you:
smoke and perfume odor
save me
leave them in peace!

Gevalt = cry for help and invocation
(yidish)

OBSESSION OF FREEDOM

I would like freedom
a few vacations
some days.

I would like vacations
get out
from myself.

I would like rest
just a little bit
not being anymore myself.

I would like to get out
of my identity
to escape, even for one time
from the obsession.

I would like
some serenity
look at me from the side
observe me from outside.

I would like God to grant me
a break
of my nightmares,
of myself.

Peter Hargitai

THE ART OF TAXIDERMY

Look for a blackbird on live wire
Mistaking it for a branch. Make
Sure it's the one whose feathers
Glint blue but only for a second
Before sparks singe the bird beak
And breathe out the animal smell.

Take the worm from the mouth
And lop off the starry comb.
Save the wings to be crucified.
Toss the innards to a whiskered
Catt. Leave the hear. Inflate with
Air till clouds sail by. Cool.
Stretch and pin the wings.
Stand upright. Spread the arsenic
Like fine-needle frost to the skin.

Continue to bloat the body
Until the heart is profoundly still.
Tear out the heart. Aerate.
Impregnate the sinus where the
Heart has been with empty air.
Hot air. Cold air. A dead blackbird
Doesn't care. Stuff it with empty
dreams. Shreds of dreams or
Shredded dreams. Random stuff
Littering the sky. Scattered
Cool and distant. But hallowed
In the unvacuumed night of stars.

And when the green and marble
Eyes, cooler than glass,
Warm up the self-
Illuminating body, it is time.

When the eyes flicker
Like glowworm
It is time to serve the body.

Peter Magliocco

OLD SONGS FOR A DESERT SUNSET

Old barren land bears no symphony
For the endangered inhabitants there,
& wizened sage branches decay.
As snakes curl in sandy beds
       God is not with us tonight.
We have hitchhiked to nowhere & back,
All across this desolate heartland
Of scorpion wend, where harvests of fire
Wilt in the desert of forgotten desire.
I made a rendering of today
       On your bare cheek bone,
Tracing the cruel sun's scarring.
Yet we laughed, renting a jeep
       Out of Laughlin,
Singing made-up songs without meaning
       Or mad melody.
Driving towards Vegas, fingers snapping
       To the ineffable rhythms
We heard welling in dead Orestes' heart,
Your tongue a lyre for your late lover
Lost in the dunes, where no lyric lingers.

Robert Malouf

LOVE AND LOSS

Two dancers,
Love and loss,
Embrace, join as one,
Surrender
To the vibrating strings
Of story, life.

Tango-close,
Choreography
By joy and sorrow,
They glide swiftly,
Softly,
Across
The weathered stage
Of time.

Two dancers,
Love and loss,
Move
In mystical perfection
To ancient steps –
Rhapsodic, tragic –
Of untold yesteryears,
Unborn tomorrows,
The eternal, heavenly ballet
Only true lovers
Know.

Robert René Galván

COLOR OF THE SOUL

What color is the soul,
ineffable waft
sealed into flesh
by a dervish
of sand?

Is it truly
the white
milk of God's
grace,
progressing
to black
with each
transgression,
or rather,
like the radiance
of the symbiont
orchid,
its tendrils
clasping
the body
for passage,
or is it an aura
that turns
with each moment,
the nebula
hosted by the
wary chameleon,
or perhaps

it is invisible,
like the residue
of a plucked
string,
a migrant tone
in the darkness?

Robin M Buehler

SHORES OF LORILEI

We were drawn to the sea
Just my brother and me
To the shores of Lorilei
The tall tails the tide brought in
of every ship, every skipper within
We lads could only drew nearer
The sailors' words we could only hear.
Entangled now by the nets the sailors weaved,
We lads could no longer leave
Now, forever bound to neither land or sea,
our lives will forever be

Ron Riekki

LOVE (FLARF)

love is more than just the way you feel,
love encompasses,

two otters that lost their partners find love,
"Real Kind of Love,"

Jennifer Aniston helps spread Wausau woman's message of love,
love is the most powerful emotion,

love is more than a feeling,
music you love,

what is love,
another word for love,

love (third-person singular simple present)
love is one of the most profound emotions known to human beings,

they were both in love with her,
Love (2015),

the "depth" of love is to be explained in terms of a notion of identification,
the 5 Love Languages ®

distinguish loving from liking via the intuition,
love has a certain charm to it,

Love's Travel Stops & Country Stores
Sex Toys Superstore

Singles in Lady Lake
Love Spell to Bring Back an Ex

Scarlett Cunningham

LIVING ROOM THEOPHANIES DURING PANDEMIC

Words leap from the page, downloading
the divine one word at a time to crucify flesh in strips.
And I kneel before the great wall of contemplation,
You lick the wounds behind my closed lids,
I purr, stroke one black cat, one gray, bathing
on overstuffed couch, rolling each syllable
for flavor, savoring the extra salt.
Surely, oh surely, you are in the purr.
Download complete, self-image-skyrockets,
imagination explodes flooding too fast.
Start over again. Crunch and toss in wastebasket.
Backspace--can't delete you.

(I am your olive. Crush me again please.)
Tears stream as newscaster transports us
in different dimension. Can't connect.

I am followed room to room. Remember the presence
in the panic room when the water heater caught fire?
No bodied presence nuzzles through alley cats
slinking in from the storm to curl before fire.
In fetal position I warm in a cocoon of rapture
rising only to kneel, pen dripping with ink as the
world outside explodes.

Susan Signe Morrison

CATHEDRAL

In Paris at the Rodin Museum
there is a smallish model
of two hands,
held erect
and facing one another,
curved and rounded,
in a Gothic arch,
creating a quiet sanctuary
between barely touching fingertips.

Just so, we flee to our refuge
where allegro slows to adagio
filling time with eternal
looks and speech and touch.

Tommy Tick

SUBLIME HERO

Only when the painter
removes the masking tape
do I see that
I'm a line
zipping through the colorfield
of red
and though I might imagine
houses
trees
and cars
they're all made of reserve lines
just as empty as I am
In them, I have no lasting city
and when I really understand these things
this absurd and endless colorfield
can be my own red studio

Victoria Crawford and George R. Ross
STUBBORN BUDDHA

You left your palace, wife, son, father, mother
To find the answer to your deepest question:
If loss and pain are part of life, why suffer?
Could it be that dukkha is an option?

You joined the five ascetics in search of truth,
their harsh fasting consumed you to the core
but gave no light—Ah! Emaciated youth!
You left the forest, becoming Mara's whore.

When neither want nor plenty quenched your thirst,
stubborn you sat under the bodhi tree
until the memes of I, Mine and Self burst,
extinguishing dukkha and setting you free.

At last you found the noble Middle Way:
be not Desire's slayer nor her slave,
    and keep the self at bay,
for self is born of ignorance and greed:
stop its birth, and Nirvana will succeed.

William Miller

DEAF CHILD

The sign is still there,
but she's gone.

After they put it up,
she played jump rope
in the street,
jacks, hopscotch.

But her mother's boyfriend
beat her mother up;
the police siren flashed.

She had to move
to another house
where the sign
was never put up.

She didn't play outside
and slept a lot,
played only with her
stuffed animals.

The siren flashed again,
and though she
didn't hear
her mother's screams,
she clapped her hands
to her ears.

Wing Yau

MOTHER, DON'T PUSH ME OUT PLEASE, DON'T

Because no one there is ready for a bad ending. Look around you —
People running in undersized shoes; tightened belts
around the waists, tripping over motherless tongues
just to understand each other. They do not say *good morning*
to the faces scrambling in the last overnight train. Their faces
scrambled on a hot oiled engine, every orifice mangle shut,
a close-up of violence framed in the quiet carriage.

Don't push me out — even if you have only one opening left.
You who had been exiled from your mummy's inside
should know better. You think you'll give me a pair of gumboots
for a head start. You think you'll tell me these shoes can protect
toes against acid, and I'll trust them like I trust your words
until I can no longer take them off when liquefied earth
is spurting out between my toes. It is never easy

to remove what used to fit. Like roots.
I'm not ready to cross that bridge
guarded by the mute *Mang Por* whose only job
is to hand out the soup to forget. I can't forget the words
I have not yet used in my past lives. I am not ready
to sway my arms like a leafless tree for balance in the wind
just to evolve, to work, to find love.

Look around you, Mother, see the man who set himself
on fire by the bridge? He'll become a homeless ghost like us
with elongated tongue on the window pane for a taste of air.

Mother, don't tell anyone how much of our ankle or chin
is left. Tell me what a lifetime is in one breath.
For our kind of horror story is no longer needed
for them to sleep at night. This is no exorcism. We will

soon be strangers again, each hiding under a different doormat
or on an elevator ceiling screaming headlessly our reincarnated
names. So let me hang on to this ball of yarn, or at least
in an obscure place like a poem forever in a blue nightgown.
Because in their world, no morning coffee will get anyone
out of their corner, or anywhere at all with a bright red
Exit sign.

Ben Gaa

country breeze
the causal scent
of cow patties

fish and chips
the hop-trot-hop
of hungry finches

new widow
all eyes on the lines of her
new corvette

evening heat
the slow shake
of the koi's tail

pulled along
with the old creek's current
our conversation

dandelion breeze
the resplendent floof
of the neighbor's cat

wandering alone
i follow the cloud's
shadow

not knowing how to let go
silence at the end
of the zoom

tonight's rain
slow and steady
the old blues tune

milkweed blossom
the open-close-open
of butterfly wings

Bryan Rickert

patchwork tweed
the near symmetry
of geese in flight

a chicken thigh
slides into the grease
noon heat

launching against the wind
a gull stuck in
place

sheltering in place
the empty park
full of birds

summer ballpark
the long hang time
of a day moon

their amble
from town to town
prairie clouds

after the swat
the fly's
crooked flight

dry creek bed
the ebb and flow
of locust song

not a tatter
on the first rose
morning dew

January thaw
the gate latch frozen
with rust

David Watts

clouds blown away
the universe
crowds the sky

morning fog
the shape
of fog

fallen roof
vortex
in the hourglass

view lost
tree trunks
behind the new fence

tide withdraws
our secret
revealed

Doc Drumheller

GUANGZHOU CITY HAIKU

one day layover
in the five goat city
luck and good fortune

the breakfast buffet
at the free hotel was fit
for an Emperor

after days of rain
a woman pours her green tea
into the gutter

year of the monkey
see no evil, hear no evil,
speak no evil

each new cycle
always starts with dragons
ending with a dog

year of the dog
why haven't I heard any
barking at the moon

master artisan
pine trees and mountaintops
painted with his palm

Chuang Tzu butterfly
flits around Tai Chi ladies
waving golden fans

city of flowers
roots under the earth sprout
the mall of the world

insects in the trees
next to the construction site
cicada saw blades

the TV Tower
Canton's slim-waisted lady
wearing garter belts
Cantonese dinner
a lazy Susan of fried
dim sum phoenix claws

after months of floods
this humid city smells
of fish and leather

a dragon boat sleeps
on a pearl river canal
green as a jade snake

in Guangzhou City
our tour guide keeps on saying
in Guangzhou City

John J. Han

FACE MASKS: SENRYU

1
wearing a face mask
or not—
that is the question

2
election day
picking between two masks—
red or blue

3
pandemic year
shaving cream lasts
much longer

4
sudden awakening—
my mask doesn't match
my outfit

5
eyes narrow above a mask—
either smiling
or scowling

6
almost mad
at someone wearing
a clear mask

7
bringing joy
to the otherwise sad day—
a cat face mask

8
turning 65—
he now wears
2 masks

9
uncertain days
eyeglasses fog up
above a mask

10
pandemic
wandering the backyard
maskless

John McDonald

auld daunce studio -
the wrackin-baw's sweeng
feshes the hoose doon

old dance studio -
the wrecking-ball's swing
fetches the house down

#
watterside poorhoose -
they gove it thirsels
aneath the watter

riverside hostel -
they gaze at themselves
beneath the water

#
furst the ambulance
wins in - syne bawdrons
his bell tinglin

first the ambulance
arrives - then cat
his bell tingling

#
magnolias apenin -
anither year
anither caunle

magnolias opening -
another year
another candle

\#
efter the beerial
tea it the gowf club
...tentie o thaim sinkin putts

after the burial
tea at the golf club
...watching them sinking putts

\#
mornin Mass -
ootby a flocht o maws
threepin in tungs

morning Mass -
outside a flurry of gulls
speaking in tongues

\#
unner the aipple tree
the auld sodger dwams
...amang the faw'n yins

under the apple tree
the old soldier dreams
...among the fallen ones

\#
hern speirin
wi ilk fuitstap
...as the bodach daes

heron probing
with each footstep
...as the old man does

\#
skateperk
hauflins makkin
dunts an birses

skatepark
youngsters making
bumps and bruises

\#
jivin
granfaither an grandochter
...tuba an clarinet wyvein

jiving
grandfather and grand-daughter
...tuba and clarinet weaving

Maya Daneva

***

cutting my finger
I remember
her sharp tongue

***

an indoor cactus
the dead fly
on the pins

***

smell of matches
lighting my candle
at the foot of the cross

***

winter deepens
how fatter now
the snowflakes

***

pink moon
the smell of honeysuckles
in her hair

***

black moon
he gives her a handful
of blackberries

***

gone one year
still learning to live with
the autumn drizzle

***

covid-sick
the rotting planks
in my rooftop

***

first date
the love for hot sauce forms
the common ground

***

an open urn
impregnating
the silence

Prof. Moshé Liba

if they say what they say
that's does not mean
that they mean what they say

the ministers do not mean
what they say
when they say: peace

you should not explain
what you
did not say

life is the best party
I have ever
being invited to

speaking about movies
something finally
is not moving there

the dream
the state of the dream
the dream for a state

from dreams forge reality
difficulties are incentives
for achievements

this soldier stands for what?
indeed he stands
to attention

189 when I am only
the feet
I do the walking

190 this man is rich
without very good manners
he cannot have also esthetics

Nicholas M. Sola

garden stroll—
turning leaves
the color of her areolas

under turning leaves
yoga poses
for the photographer

hillside bus stop
her hands warmed
by a can of coffee

winter morning
the line outside
the pachinko parlor

old pond—
pine needles
comb my hair

out of the child's reach apples in the orchard

overlooking the ocean
oranges on a hill
behind an electric fence

smiling at the moon
the old man
with rotten teeth

streets of Jinbocho—
do the books know
that it is winter?

Thanksgiving
the gold plate
in the microwave

Samo Kreutz

1.>
village street
coming and going
the morning wind

2.>
melting ice
all the vehicles
iridescent

3.>
children outside
freshly fallen snow
no longer alone

4.>
winter silence
holding him in her arms
deep melancholia

5.>
hunting season
among trees bleeds
the evening sun

6.>
macadam road
embracing the stars
only dust

Santosh Kumar

ruthless brutality on earth
the innocent among assassins:
we are unworthy of lord's love

attention at its fullest
praying to avert nuclear war:
tibetan buddhist yogi

glorious treasure house:
enjoying eternity in each moment
living in the present

sunshine of our lives
my sure support
little singing bird

hemingway strong at broken places
enlightened by tribulation
in our corrupted time

devil comes with bitter ends
coronavirus strikes earth
no rest but in blessed love

even on darkest hour
peace of mind
within olive grove of grace

aspiring to salvation
filling cups with holy water
as mysterious deity's meals

underneath bodhi tree
buddha weeps:
nuclear warfare

blazing violets
touch monk's feet:
birth of zen

WORLD LITERATURE QUIZ
QUESTIONS AND ANSWERS

Questions:

1.   Who won the Pulitzer Prize four times?

2.   Who is the Father of English poetry?

Answers:

1. Robert Frost

2. Geoffrey Chaucer

ATTENTION POETS!!

BOOK PUBLISHING

Publishing a manuscript rewards the author in several ways. The wide review of the book will certainly establish the author's fame in the world of letters. A literary prize or a fellowship may be awarded to the artist, whose compositions will be appreciated by innumerable magazines.

If you are interested in finding a publisher for your book, Cyberwit will work closely with you in publishing books of fiction and non-fiction, including: novels, short stories, poems, biographies, autobiographies, psychology, religion, history, health, humor etc. We have published a great number of new writers. Further details are available from :

Karunesh Kumar Agrawal
www. cyberwit.net/ email: info@cyberwit.net
Ph.+91.9415091004

BOOK
REVIEWS

Three Plays by Aristophanes Review – Sarah Mackey Kirby (Impspired) (As directed by Gary Beck)

Publisher : Cyberwit.net (September 21, 2020)

Language: : English Paperback : 257 pages

ISBN-13 : 978-9390202935

In Aristophanes, Beck and Oliensis bring creativity and wit to three of the Ancient Greek playwright's comedies. The book comprises three plays: The Women in Assembly, The Birds, and Lysistrata. Their translations animate the political satire and antics laden plots characteristic of his writing. And while reading these, it's easy to picture and feel life in the polis. While the plots have a heavy dose of absurdity (in a good way), that absurdity serves to enlighten the audience and criticize the powers that be about war, political events, and everyday Athens.

The first play, The Women in Assembly, follows Praxagora on her scheme to put women in charge of the Athenian government. Beck and Oliensis capture the reforms she wants instituted. As the play unfolds, readers and audiences are immersed in how Athenian government works and the roles of women and men in society (and how changes to it could change life in Athens). There is a tangible energy that shines through.

In The Birds, the second play translation, Pisthetaerus and his friend, Euelpides set out to find the former Thracian King Tereus who'd transformed into Epops, a hoopoe bird and King of the Birds. Having become frustrated with Athens, they wanted wisdom and guidance about where to go to begin life anew. The events and exchanges leading to their meeting him are very funny, and the two men come up with the idea that the birds should create their own city in the sky because it is they (the birds) and not the Olympic Gods who are divine.

The play continues as a farcical and captivating story that is enjoyable until the end. The Chorus, typical to Old Comedy structure, elevates the play. This translation does justice to Aristophanes and his gift with satire, and the pictures of the bird costumes they include after the script add to it.

In the last play, Beck and Oliensis translate Lysistrata. With the goal of saving Greece by ending war (the Peloponnesian War), Lysistrata convinces women in Athens and in other city-states, including Sparta, to join together and refuse sex to all men until they stop fighting. The play goes on to show what happens after the women agree. This play, anti-war and rich with satire, brings sharp humor and undertones of seriousness. However, the sexual content is pervasive throughout, so performing the play may be a bit more challenging than the first two.

Readers and no doubt audiences to a staged production, should enjoy these lively and funny plays. Aristophanes is a collection of quality translations that bring to life the Ancient Greek playwright's wonderful works of classic comedy.

BROADWAY FOR PAUL By Vincent Katz

Publisher : Knopf (April 7, 2020)

Language: : English

Hardcover : 144 pages

ISBN-10 : 052565657X

ISBN-13 : 9780525656579

Vincent Katz is the author of the poetry collections Southness (2016) and Swimming Home (2015) and of the book of translations The Complete Elegies of Sextus Propertius (2004), which won a National Translation Award from the American Literary Translators Association. He is the editor of Black Mountain College: Experiment in Art (2002), and his writing on contemporary art and poetry has appeared in publications such as Apollo, Art in America, ARTnews, The Brooklyn Rail, and The Poetry Project Newsletter. As curator of the "Readings in Contemporary Poetry" series at Dia:Chelsea, Katz also edited the anthology Readings in Contemporary Poetry (2017). He lives in New York City.

It is stunning that Vincent won a National Translation Award from the American Literary Translators Association for his book The Complete Elegies of Sextus Propertius.

With the title, BROADWAY FOR PAUL, this book is a compilation of several aesthetic poems. The art of showing the glimpses from the poet's point of view is remarkable in most of the poems. Vincent's wonderous and wise perspective amuses the reader's mind and creates joy in the reader's heart also.

The opening poem, 'BETWEEN THE GRIFFON AND MET LIFE,' in its beginning only captivates the reader. "I am totally enamored of every person passing in this unseasonably warm mid-March evening", the word 'enamored' shows an immense feeling of love in the poet's heart for every passing person who is a stranger.

BETWEEN THE GRIFFON AND MET LIFE

I am totally enamored of every person passing in this unseason-
ably warm mid-March evening near 39th and Park
The young women, of course, with their lives in front of them, and

*the young men too, just standing here as I am, checking it out,
hanging out, talking
But everyone here, every age, every type, is beautiful, the moment, somehow, the weather, has made them all real and for this
moment, before it turns to night, they're all fantastic
The light is such that I can see everyone and can imagine what
they are imagining for the night ahead, what dreams, what ful-
filled fantasies of togetherness
And the two guys who were here a moment ago, paused, have
moved on, and the light is deepening, every moment or so, actually falling into a deeper stupor, which is night
But if I look south I still see the pink flush of desire there at the
bottom, the southness of all our lives, and it's okay that it's
darkening here, people accept it as they concoct plans for tonight, Thursday
Soon I'll have to go too, lose this spot, this moment, but some
we've met and some experience we had somewhere else is becoming ever more important*

While reading BROADWAY FOR PAUL, one gets the impression that the poet is telling his story as he has lived it, in his own words and in his own way, with an insertion of various fantasies.

In '7 A.M. POEM,' the poet describes the quotidian routine of people. "They have work to do and they are trying to do it / Families to feed and teach", symbolizes the struggle and effort of the people, who do work to satisfy their wants and needs.

7 A.M. POEM

*They carry their lunches in paper or plastic bags
They are rushing but composed
They don't speak much
They're quiet this morning, maybe preoccupied with big violent
forces moving in the capital
They have work to do and they are trying to do it
Families to feed and teach or else
Just moving ahead with life, trying to be someplace better
A little further on ahead*

The people arriving on trains are not New Yorkers, but
They too are filled with desires, plans, wrapped in winter coats
As the people crashed out on stairs or in abandoned buildings
People in high boardrooms creating situations affecting those
with nothing

In 'BEGINNING OF THE PICNIC,' the words 'breezes / Keep air moving… //

sunlight on leaves… // afternoon lingers…' showcase the inherent beauty of nature.

Moreover, it appears to be that the poet is in search of an atmosphere where he can write poetry.

BEGINNING OF THE PICNIC

Let's see if I can write some poetry now
It doesn't look like it, sitting on the veranda
Above a quiet street, a Tuesday at
Year's beginning, warm, sunlight on leaves

Rainfall earlier cleared out but clouds
Returned, yet all is lush and breezes
Keep air moving in and out, below
 Two men walk past, conversing

A garage door slides open, a car backs out,
Birds cackle nearby, dogs farther off
Resound, the car returns, the door slides,
The car slips in, afternoon lingers

This collection by Vincent Katz reveals flamboyant imagery and vigorousness in his poems, which show original accents and lively imagination. I find that his poetic style is lucid, succinct, and fluent. I can surely give a green signal to potential readers that this book is worth buying. I hope that in the future I will get more books by Vincent to review. To be honest I am overwhelmed after reading this book……..

Rochak Agarwal

Fortune Written On Wet Grass By Eileen Mish Murphy

Publisher : Wapshott Press; Illustrated edition (February 5, 2020)

Language: : English Paperback : 62 pages

The radiant poems in Eileen Mish Murphy's latest poetic collection "Fortune Written on Wet Grass" are prototypical undoubtedly. There has been a great diffusion of natural beauty among all the poems. Most of the poems portray the true inherent exquisiteness of rain and flowers. There is a prolific description of human beings, plants, flowers, and rainy weather which is quite remarkable as well as soothes the reader's mind. Quite a few noteworthy poems in this remarkable collection flash true insights of the moments of rainy weather.

The opening poem, Fortune Written on Wet Grass, reveals a wonderful conversation between rain and the poet. The line 'rain talking to me' has a great significance of its own. It gives a huge increment in the euphoria of the reader and the way of personifying is really impressive and looks amazing.

Fortune Written on Wet Grass

All over Florida,

it's drizzling

with dazzling monotony.

The rain is warm

as a baby's breath

and a sweat drop drools

down the middle

of my shirt

and cradles

itself in my cleavage

and I hear

the rain

talking to me—
it says
I should lose
ten pounds,
clean out my sewers,
comb my lawn,
learn jazz piano,
and spruce up
this rinky-dink operation—
Hey, rain,
can ya hear me?
I don't mind
being a recluse:
I'm not leaving
this porch—

In The Rain Has Lost Its Mind, the poet aptly expresses the ferocious behaviour of rain because of which 'Fireflies explode in the night/ Elephants trample the clouds'. 'Dog hides in the bathtub' symbolizes a typical rainy weather. 'I' m just a wee creature/I find oil lamps/and coax the dog/into their light' these lines show common acts carried out by people when the weather suddenly gets worse. The poem showcases a typical raining scenario, experienced by the poet.

In The Color of Waiting, the poet shows her curiosity for the tulip bulb to bloom 'as we don't know how long/the bursting/will take.' The poem looks beautiful and flashes the beauty of the tulips' bulb. How one wouldn't linger on such a line 'But tulips in pots/on the porch /take their sweet time'? Sweetness, ecstasy, and elation are the very words to describe this wonderful poem.

The Color of Waiting

Use blue as a symbol for the time
it takes a tulip bulb
to burst into bloom.
A paint swatch on paper

is more compelling
than a number—

we don't know how long
the bursting
will take.

Tulips
in the ground
will first
send up shoots,

Eileen's poem Nocturne, Catnip and Rain Again shows her remarkable range and vision. She shows her love for nature in her poetry in a well-sophisticated way. Her poems are enlivened by lively intelligence, fascinating natural creatures and evocative experiences. This remarkable poetic collection deserves a lot of love and support from the readers. I wish that author may get exposure along with this book. All the best Eileen!

Rochak Agarwal

Review of *ngâ whakamatuatanga/interludes* by Vaughan Rapatahana, Published by Cyberwit, Allahabad, India

ngâ whakamatuatanga/interludes is the latest collection of poems by the New Zealand Mâori poet Vaughan Rapatahana. As in previous poetry collections such as *Home Away, Elsewhere* (Proverse, Hong Kong), and *Atonement* (University of Santo Tomas Press, Philippines) the content of the collection reflects Rapatahana's peripatetic lifestyle and his well-received poetry publications in Hong Kong, Macau, Philippines, USA, England, France and New Zealand.

Rapatahana is a strong critic of the domination of English in countries where other languages were traditionally spoken by the original inhabitants. To this end, he has inaugurated and co-edited *English Language as Hydra* and *Why English? Confronting the Hydra* (Multilingual Matters, U.K. 2012 and 2016).

ngâ whakamatuatanga/interludes is a bilingual collection of poems in te reo Mâori and English. The poems in this collection display a range of intense emotions. They are at times angry, and sardonic, at times ironic and spirited. Metaphors and similes abound in the collection, as well as the clash between English and te reo Mâori.

As it is published in India, Rapatahana's collection will no doubt remind Indian readers that English is the second most known language in India after Hindi. There are 22 official languages in the 28 Indian states. 11 states have English as their official language or as an additional official language. In 2014, the historian Sandeep Bhardwaj published a book on India's national languages with the title *Hindi, English or Nothing: Politics of India's National Languages.*

Unlike previous poetry collections by Rapatahana, this anthology is divided into 6 sections with bilingual titles: (i) *ngâ wâhi/places*; (ii) *ngâ whakamatuatanga/relationships; (iii) te ao tûroa/ nature; (iv) ngâ tôrangaûu raua ko ngâ rapunga whakairo/ politics and philosophy, (v) ngâ toikupu/poetry* and *(vi) te raro/the underworld.* The ambiance of the poems is sometimes lighthearted but in other cases dark and poignant.

More, as with most of Vaughan Rapatahana's work, the content of this collection often consists of "shape" or "concrete" poems. The typographical arrangement of words is as important to meaning as the conventional elements of poetry such as word meaning, rhythm, rhyme and imagery. Capital letters and punctuation are largely ignored. In the poem *te araroa foreshore, mid-winter* **(pages 10-11)** , the poet sees his presence thus:

& as for me

I am but an a f t e r t h o u g h t

a drifter gathering driftwood,

the fictionalized version

of myself

s h i p w r e c k e d

amongst the sea wrack

as dusk drowns

my way

Similes and metaphors appear in the text with powerful and surprising images, often accompanied by rarely used words ("telluric", "scurfy"...)

Waitangi 2017 (pages 6 and 7)

as sunrise sulks

behind sentry clouds

refusing to grant us grace

we traipse telluric

that scurfy scrub

enduring h e r e & t h e r e

like scabrous cur

too stubborn to die

The first group of the collection, "places", includes the weather ("gone troppo", "mid-winter" and "a winter's day"). Everyday places describe waiting for a train, taking the last bus and a dangerous route in Manila:

best route to batangas (pages 16-18)

O.K. claim a lane,

fastest pedal wins,

\-   gotta have that

magic swerve

\-   gonna be the one

without nerve

while the zapping synapses

divagate

t h r o u g h their brains

Some of other places in the section involve darker events:

mô ôtautahi 2019 for Christchurch 2019, (**pages 21-22**), lamenting the massacre of Muslims in two mosques:

me kâore tçtahi ki te mate i roto i te are taua

kâore tçtahi

no one needs to die in such a way

no one

vietnam days, (pages 29-31), detailing the Aotearoa/New Zealand population's attitude to their participation in the war:

was protesting the war

in 1972

it was a schismatic year

as I opposed our troops

battling in phuoc tuy

& got abused by

my fellow countrymen

who eulogized americans

Aotearoa New Zealand, (pages 23-26) discusses the necessity of a new name for the nation:

with our increasingly multi-cultural crew

Pâkehâ, Mâori, Asian, Pasifika –

is it time for a new name,

stressing our interconnections?

after all we are rowing together

In the poem **within (pages 32-33),** Rapatahana expresses his anguish at the "dying" houses where many Mâori families live:

within

the roof was a falsehood

as it imploded the ceiling

& the walls cried out

In mutual agony

Rangiaowhia 1864 (pages 34-36) relates an act of savagery carried out by British troops against the residents of Rangiaowhia in 1864:

who knows about the murders at Rangiaowhia?

not the majority of this country nowadays.

who remembers the burned children?

not the majority in this district.

(ii) ngâ *whakamatuatanga/relationships* consists of three wildly passionate love poems, **she, if it had ben love…** and **inhabit.** This is followed by family relationships, the poet's father, his lost son, his own role as a father to his Asian daughter-in-law, and to a school supervisor:

father was a white man

my father was a fight man

the only war he ever fought

was the punch-up in the bedroom;

the audience of kids

suffocating the bedclothes in their fear

of the ruckus next door, resounding

through those thin walls.

The supervisor, as in other places where colonizing languages dominate, makes sure that the language spoken by the original inhabitants is stamped out, particularly in the schools:

the supervisor called

the supervisor roared

                          me

i n t o her den

as I was strolling by

appropriateness, timeliness

castigated me for speaking in

my own language the day before

(iii) te ao tûroa/nature

In this section, nature and the weather are personified, sometimes as happy, friendly people:

good old summer

summer came back

with

a HUGE grin

s p r e a d e a g l e d

all over its face

the afternoon

the afternoon

turned to me,

conspiratorial,

speaking of ill winds

Autumn on the other hand, is compared to a feral dog:

autumn

autumn grovels in;

like a demented mongrel,

sly,   *l e a n*

                                & mean

These images remind us of other personifications by Rapatahana, for example in *Atonement* we read

the rain

    struts past

my window

like a petulant dog

The other weather poems in this section are clearly described in the titles:

death in winter; today kills; this day is a dog and **under the weather**

Section (iv) *ngâ tôrangaûu raua ko ngâ rapunga whakairo/ politics and philosophy* starts with political dispute in the poem **debatable.** The poem **robert mugabe is dead (pages 95-97)** consists of an overview of the current political "leaders" of the world and their wished-for fate: dead, impeached, in solitary, behind bars in Siberia, a refugee in Australia, excess of drugs, a short order cook, plastic surgery …. until the next one "usurps the throne"

In **I'm having trouble with words (pages 100-101)**, Rapatahana revisits the English/Mâori issue:

I'm having trouble with words

you know

    the usual ones

      the english ones,

they bloviate me

in their revanchist fury.

NB Its not as if Rapatahana doesn't have a command of English. *Bloviate* is a style of empty, pompous, political speech.

The term **Philosophy** leads us to the poem **ko te mutunga o te atua (the end of god)**

so god ends here:

yet the question remains,

did god ever commence?

whose god is this anyway

& what do they mean by it?

(v) ngâ toikupu/poetry In these poems, Rapatahana looks at the various ways of creating poetry. First of all, writing poetry isn't easy:

sometimes (pages 113-114)

sometimes

writing a poem

is like

driving

      a   u

              n

   bus   d

               e

             r

    w a t e r

A poem is not a fixed body. It can be speech, where the poet can "breathe the poem". The poem can also spring out "like one of those north korean warheads". In the poem **on the occasions of reading for p.e.n."** **(pages119-120)** Rapatahana asserts that "verdant trees dancing beneath scudding clouds" or "lost love" are pointless topics when compared to "kiribati is sinking steadily into the sea" or "kids continue to live in cars in winter".

The collection ends with a short section **(vi) te raro/the underworld.** Two of the poems are nefarious, if not sinister: **suppressed images, too vile to share (pages 128-130)** and **koromiko suicide (pages 131-133).** A koromiko is a small tree or a shrub in Aotearoa/New Zealand used as a medicine. (The suicide reminds us of Van Gogh, who shot himself in a wheat field.)

Ironically, the last poem can be seen as less bleak: **I want a good death (pages 134-135)**

laughing untrammelled

as my fingers untwine

from loved one's grip

& my eyes greet   what   is

                              next

on the list.

Although *ngâ whakamatuatanga/interludes* has similarities with previous collections by Vaughan Rapatahana, the interludes, or "intermissions", provide a series of "chapters" which allow the reader to predict (more or less) the gist of each episode. The poems in most cases contain strong feelings but they cannot be called "lyrical": in many cases they tend to be disapproving. The poems are more in the line of narration. Something is always happening, for example the weather, which is seen as a living thing, good or bad. *ngâ whakamatuatanga/ interludes* is a powerful and multi-faceted reflection on places, relationships, nature, politics and philosophy, poetry and the underworld...wherever it is.

Alan Chamberlain

Taj Mahal Review International Journal Authors: Various Worldwide

Page Length: 168 Pages

Copyright: 2019

Date Published: December 2019

Language: English

Sold by: www.cybetwit.net

ISSN: 0972-6004

Reviewer: Joseph S. Spence Sr.

Introduction:

Taj Mahal Review International Journal is an excellent publication of short stories, regular poems, haiku poems, book reviews, and interviews. It was founded in 2002, in Allahabad, India, and is devoted to the cause of poetic articulation for the planet to be a better place to live. It asked poets to be stimulated by visual and auditory imagery; thus, revealing a remarkable variety of life, and to display blended faith with healthy skepticism. It desires its publications to reflect a post-modern trend, without obscurity, artificiality, and violation of laws of criticism. It does not accept compositions founded on violent self-pity or feelings of egocentricity.

Short Stories Section:

The short story selected to review is by Dr. Sourya Acharya, titled "The Story Teller," which is very intriguing and highlights the following:

He had escaped from the quagmire of chaos, finally to caress his fatigue brain, stimulate it, and rejuvenate it for the perfect story he wanted to create. This story would epitomize a renaissance. He used to wander through mountains, rivers, deserts, oceans, telling stories to the trees, snow, days, nights, rocks, creatures, birds, angels, and ghosts, and they were amazed by his stories. A great storyteller has to be a great listener and listen in silence. He escaped from the quagmire of chaos, finally to this most prolonged vacuum of his soul. It's here he realized he will open his stories. The clouds will listen to the stories of mountains. The ocean will listen to the stories of the wind. The snow will listen to the stories of the sand. The ghosts will listen to the stories of the soulless. And, as a superb storyteller, his legacy will travel through eternity for births to come in eternal silence!

Regular Poetry Section:

The first poem selected for review is D. C. Buschmann's poem titled, "Family." It's is very inspiring. Experts follow:

>Community of voices
>>a melodious chorus
>>sopranos, alto, tenor, bass
>
>Distinctive
>>pitches and ranges
>>resonate harmony
>
>Without each voice
>>the whole, incomplete
>>leaving the un-whole
>>a mere cacophony

Here our inspiration author highlights the value of his community as an integrated successful whole and not singular failing parts.

The next selected poem is titled "Kinship." Authored by Gary Beck, it presents a comparative analysis of cities in the Western and Eastern Worlds. Excerpts follow:

>The cities in the Western world
>Have cancerous slums, consume millions.
>Far removed from wealthy neighborhoods
>Business districts, entertainment areas
>Creating an illusion that poverty doesn't exist.
>
>The cities in the Western world
>Have pandemic slums, consume tens of millions
>Spill their denizens into of poor, ragged, hungry, diseased
>Into wealthy neighborhoods, business districts
>Shattering the illusion that poverty doesn't exist.

This analysis shows the difference in the classification of slums and their impact on society in their worldwide jurisdictions.

The next poem, "I Return," authored by Moshe Liba, sends a different image of life as follows:

> I return
> To the editor,
> My pen.
> To the army,
> My weapons.
> To the woman,
> My children.
> My wife.
> To God,
> My soul
>
> I return.

Our impressive author reflects on what's essential in his life to which he has returned for inspirational upliftment.

Haiku Poetry Section:

The next section of this inspiration journal is about haiku poems. This first one selected is written by Albert Russo, titled "Mannahata." It reads:

> Twenty years of absence!
> How I fear our encounter!
> How would I react?

Our uplifting author reflects on how physical non-presence impacts the soul just as a physical presence. The reactions from both are usually a mind searching experience.

Following this mind questioning haiku poem of absence is a series of haiku poems by Ben Moeller-Gaa. The most inspiring and realistic one follows:

> Happy hour
> The loosened ties
> Of salesmen

This haiku reflects reality in its most accurate form. One can see this stunning imagery, especially of Friday evenings at a pub after work.

John McDonald's authors, the third haiku poem. The two most inspirational verses regarding reality state:

Her white communion dress
    Her golden ponytail
    …a lit candle

    At that age now:
    Walking in the night
    Checking each other's breathing

The coronavirus pandemic has impacted worldwide humanity. The act of checking on each other's breathing carries a sense of urgency for survival.

Santosh Kumar, the distinguished editor, penned a most uplifting haiku of realization as follows:

Heaven and earth rejoice

As we discover

Fountains of peace are within

Many have looked for inspiration and happiness outside. Kumar lets the world knows such attributes are innately generated.

Gems of Thoughts Section:

This next section of this inspiring Journal is titled "Gems of Thoughts." It relates to thoughts from historic figures of literary importance. The most uplifting one is from E. E. Cummings, which states:

I thank you, God, for most this amazing day:
For the leaping greenly spirits of trees
And a true-blue dream of sky; and for everything
Which is natural, which is infinite, which is yes!

Here Cummings renders thanks to God for nature. That which is refreshing, free, brings natural inspiration and is required for life's survival.

Book Review and Interview Section:

The Journal ends with several book reviews and an inspiring interview conducted by the director of "Semanario Hebreo." This interview took place in Jerusalem with the dynamic Dr. Moshe Liba, Director General of the Central Institute of Cultural Relations with Israel, Ibero, America, Spain, and Portugal. It's a very inspiring and thought-provoking interview.

Taj Mahal Journal is a very composite narration of short stories, regular and haiku poems, book reviews, and interviews across the spectrum, for one's reading pleasure. There is something for everyone's interest and reading pleasure in this text.

Have a fantastic day, don't forget to pray, stay encouraged, inspired, ingenious, resilient, mindful, and enlightened by God's grace and blessings always!

The higher reality of consciousness enhances peace, love, harmony, and happiness in our hearts with actions we connectively accomplished through faith."

– His Excellency, Ambassador, Professor, Dr. Joseph S. Spence Sr. USA (Epulaeryu Master)!

The Reviewer:

Professor Dr. Joseph S. Spence, Sr, (Epulaeryu Master), authored ten poetry books and over 200 peer-reviewed articles, and his writings appeared globally. He has membership in various international honor societies and taught at Bryant and Stratton University. He retired from the U. S. Army as an officer and received an appointment as a Goodwill Ambassador for Arkansas, USA (Commissioned by former President William Jefferson Clinton). He created "Epulaeryu," "Linking Pin Sonnet," and "Seventh Heaven" poetry forms while studying English literature, creative writing, African Diaspora, Japanese linguistics, and poetry at the University of Wisconsin. He has received numerous poetry awards worldwide and is a "Lead the Change Agent" for the University of Wisconsin, Milwaukee.

Mary Anne Zammit

Petals of Love depicts the situation of a woman who has opened her petals for love and is now protecting her heart. The medium is charcoal, acrylics with installed flowers.

Richard Hanus

AUTHOR INDEX

Alan Elyshevitz is the author of a collection of stories, The Widows and Orphans Fund (SFA Press), and three poetry chapbooks, most recently Imaginary Planet (Cervena Barva). His poems have appeared in River Styx, Nimrod International Journal, and Water ? Stone Review, among many others. Winner of the James Hearst Poetry Prize from North American Review, he is also a two-time recipient of a fellowship in fiction writing from the Pennsylvania Council on the Arts. For further information, visit https://aelyshevitz.ink.

Alessio Zanelli is an Italian poet who writes in English and whose work has appeared in some 180 literary journals from 16 countries. His fifth original collection, titled *The Secret Of Archery*, was published in 2019 by Greenwich Exchange (London). For more information please visit www.alessiozanelli.it.

Amanda Blue Leigh - poet, singer/songwriter, energy healer - Los Angles California, USA.

Andrew McIntyre has published more than 50 short stories in numerous magazines, including *Yareah Magazine, Istanbul Literary Review,* and *Catamaran Literary Reader.* He is the author of *The Short, the Long, and the Tall* (Merilang Press, 2010), a collection of 34 stories, all published between 2000 and 2010.

Ben Moeller-Gaa is a Pushcart nominated* haiku poet and author of the ***2018 Touchstone Award*** winning book, ***Wishbones*** (Folded Word 2018). He also has authored three haiku chapbooks *Fiddle in the Floorboards* (*Yavanika Press 2018), Wasp Shadows** (Folded Word 2014), and *Blowing on a Hot Soup Spoon* (poor metaphor 2014). His poems, reviews and essays have appeared in over 50 journals worldwide including *Acorn, December, Frogpond, Modern Haiku, Shamrock, The Heron's Nest,* and *World Haiku Review* as well as in over thirty anthologies including the *Red Moon Press's* yearly "best of" anthologies, The Haiku Foundation's mobile haiku app, and *Haiku 21* an anthology of English language haiku from the first decade of the twenty first century.

Bryan Rickert lives in Belleville, Illinois. In the last number of years Bryan has been published in Frogpond, Modern Haiku, Acorn, Akitsu Quarterly, The Heron's Nest, Presence, Prune Juice, Failed Haiku, Contemporary Haibun Online, Haibun Today, Atoms of Haiku III, Horizon: The Haiku Anthology, Taj Mahal Review, Atlas Poetica, Wales Haiku, Harvest of New Millennium, The Red River Book of Haibun Vol. 1, and a number of other fine journals and anthologies. He is the editor at The Living Senryu Anthology and the Co-Editor of Failed Haiku Journal of Senryu. His poetry collection "Fish Kite" is available through Cyberwit Publishing.

David Flynn was born in the textile mill company town of Bemis, TN. His jobs have included newspaper reporter, magazine editor and university teacher. He has five degrees and is both a Fulbright Senior Scholar and a Fulbright Senior Specialist with a recent grant in Indonesia. His literary publications total more than two hundred. He currently lives in Nashville, TN, where he is director of the Musicians Reunion, an annual blues festival now in its 35th year. He also teaches at Belmont University in the English and Asian Studies programs.

David Watts is from CA, USA.

Dion O'Reilly: dionoreilly.wordpress.com

Doc Drumheller: was born in Charleston, South Carolina and has lived in New Zealand for more than half his life. He has worked in award winning groups for theatre and music and has published ten collections of poetry. His poems have been translated into more than twenty languages, and he has performed in Cuba, Lithuania, Italy, Hungary, Bulgaria, Romania, Japan, India, China, Nicaragua, USA, Mexico, El Salvador, and widely throughout NZ. He lives in Oxford, where he edits and publishes the literary journal *Catalyst*.

Don Schaeffer has previously published a dozen volumes of poetry, his first in 1996, not counting the experiments with self publishing under the name "Enthalpy Press." He spent a lot of his young adult life hawking books and learning the meaning of vanity. His poetry has appeared in numerous periodicals and has been translated into Chinese for distribution abroad. Don is a habitue of the poetry forum network and has received first prize in the Interboard (IBPC) competition.

Emiliana Russo is from Puglianello (BN) Italy.

Eric Tessier is a French writer, who writes both in French and English. He is the published author of several novels (*"L'extase du prédateur"*, *"Pauline ultime"*), poetry books and collections of short stories (*"Le vin étoilé"*, *"Fleurs de givre"*, *"The Endless Journey"*); he is also a playwright (*"Le mystère de Grisville-la-Gadoue"*). He is the editor-in-chief of a financial newsletter (*"Le.Crible"*) and has published a history of the French social security (*"Une histoire de l'Urssaf de Paris, 1948-2011"*). He is also the published author of the first biography in French of rock 'n' roll singer Alice Cooper (*"Alice Cooper, parrain du shock rock"*, éditions Camion Blanc) and of the first biography ever written of the legendary soul band Booker T & the MG's (*"Booker T and the MG's, Green Onions & Memphis Soul"*, Camion Blanc). He is a radio host (*"Place Aux Fous"* show on RL 89.4 fm, Paris). He lives in Vitry-sur-Seine, France, with his beloved wife Jacqueline and a lovely black and white cat named Xiao Shan.

Fran Shaw, Ph.D. is a university professor and an award-winning author whose books include *Notes on The Next Attention*, *Writing My Yoga: Poems for Presence*, *50 Ways to Help You Write*, and *Lord Have Murphy: Waking Up in the Spiritual Marketplace*. She is working on a short-story cycle about people's experiences at spiritual retreats. For excerpts, visit www.franshawbooks.com.

Gary Beck has spent most of his adult life as a theater director and worked as an art dealer when he couldn't earn a living in the theater. He has also been a tennis pro, a ditch digger and a salvage diver. His original plays and translations of Moliere, Aristophanes and Sophocles have been produced Off Broadway. His poetry, fiction and essays have appeared in hundreds of literary magazines and his published books include 28 poetry collections, 11 novels, 3 short story collections, 1 collection of essays and 2 books of plays. Published poetry books include: Dawn in Cities, Assault on Nature, Songs of a Clerk, Civilized Ways, Displays, Perceptions, Fault Lines, Tremors, Perturbations, Rude Awakenings, The Remission of Order, Contusions and Desperate Seeker (Winter Goose Publishing. Forthcoming: Learning Curve and Ignition Point). Earth Links, Too Harsh For Pastels, Severance, Redemption Value and Fractional Disorder (Cyberwit Publishing). His novels include Extreme Change (Winter Goose Publishing). and Wavelength (Cyberwit Publishing). His short story collections include:

A Glimpse of Youth (Sweatshoppe Publications). Now I Accuse and other stories (Winter Goose Publishing) and Dogs Don't Send Flowers and other stories (Wordcatcher Publishing). Collected Essays of Gary Beck (Cyberwit Publishing). The Big Match and other one act plays (Wordcatcher Publishing). Collected Plays of Gary Beck Volume 1 and Three Comedies by Aristophanes translated, then directed by Gary Beck (Cyberwit Publishing). Gary lives in New York City.

George K. Karos was raised in Martinsburg, West Virginia, where he attended public schools until the completion of seventh grade. He then attended and graduated from Saint James School located in Washington County, Maryland. He received his Bachelor of Arts from West Virginia University in 1991, and his Master of Arts from American University in 1999.

Gordana Radovanovic was born on 23rd August 1963 in Maribor (Slovenia). She writes poetry, haiku and short stories and up till now seven of her books have been published (four books of poetry, one book of haiku poems and two books of short stories). She writes in Serbian lnguage. She lives and works in Banja Luka (Bosnia and Herzegovina).

Greg has been a factory worker, soil tester, soldier, PR executive, and journalist. He is the author of several books including Helping Hands of the Locust People and The Pizza Diaries.

John J. Han (Ph.D., University of Nebraska-Lincoln) is Professor of English & Creative Writing and Chair of the Humanities Division at Missouri Baptist University. Han is the author, editor, co-editor, compiler, or translator of twenty-five books, including *Worlds Gone Awry: Essays on Dystopian Fiction* (McFarland, 2018), *Autumn Butterfly: Haiku, Senryu, and Other Poems* (Cyberwit, 2019), and *On the Road Again: Photo Essays on Famous Literary Sites in Japan* (Cyberwit, 2020). Han's poems have also appeared in numerous periodicals and anthologies worldwide, including the *Asahi Shimbun*, *Cave Region Review*, *drifting-sands-haibun*, *Elder Mountain*, *Frogpond*, *The Laurel Review*, the *Mainichi Shimbun*, *Mariposa*, *Modern Haiku*, *POMPA*, *The Red Moon Anthology of English-Language Haiku*, *Shot Glass Journal*, *Simply Haiku*, *South by Southeast*, *Steinbeck Studies*, *Taj Mahal Review*, *Tanka Origins*, *A Vast Sky: An Anthology of Contemporary World Haiku*, *Wales Haiku Journal*, and *World Haiku Review*.

John McDonald: "I am a retired stone-mason living in Scotland and writing in one of the two languages native to Scotland (the other being Gaelic) I came to haiku in the mid-nineties and fell in love with the genre. I have a Bi-Lingual web blog http://zenspeug.blogspot.com which I try to update daily."

Joseph S. Spence, Sr., is the author of three poetry books: "The Awakened One Poetics," "Trilogy Moments for the Mind, Body and Soul," and "A Trilogy of Poetry, Prose and Thoughts for the Mind, Body and Soul." His book, "Trilogy Moments for the Mind, Body and Soul," won the Best Christian Poetry Award from Christian Story Tellers. "The Awakened One Poetics," won 2nd place in the Critters Writers Workshop Best Author's Pool, and was also the Publisher's Best Seller. His writings have appeared in many national and international forums including: Cram 7 Chicago Poetry, Sound of Poetry Review, Möbius Poetry, Autumn Leaves, Poetinis Druskininkø, Phoenix Magazine, Harvest of New Millennium, The Rubicon, Word Catalyst, Burns Chronicle, Newspapers, U. S. Army, The Edition, and Taj Mahal Review. He has taught at Bryant and Stratton University, and retired from the U.S. Army as an officer with 20-years of service. He is a Goodwill Ambassador for the state of Arkansas, and has received many poetry awards including the following: Poetry Ambassador Medal (USA), Poetry Bard Award (UK), Who's Who in Poetry, (USA), Numerous Editor's Choice Awards (USA), and Independent Poet Laureate (USA). He embraces is paternal Scottish ancestry and is a member of the Scottish Poetry Bard, Robert Burns Club, Wisconsin.

KaZ Akers was first published at the age of fourteen in a teen magazine. Subsequently, she went on to have plays and songs published and produced, magazine articles in print and online, and short stories in book compilations and anthologies. She co-wrote two produced informational television series and two television pilots. She singularly wrote a third television situation comedy pilot. Her poetry and short stories have been published in print and online. She has written articles for women's online health and wellness magazines and is in demand for her editing skills. In addition, KaZ was a performer in television, film and on stage as a singer, dancer, actor, stunt person, circus artist and professional water skier. As an entrepreneur, she has co-owned two restaurants, a cinema, a television production company and a fitness centre. Currently, she exclusively writes short stories and poetry. KaZ is a certified master meditation instructor and third level Qigong instructor and uses those techniques to enhance her writing and to coach other writers.

Keith Moul writes poems and takes photos, doing both for more than 50 years. He concentrates on empirical moments in time, recognizing that the world will be somewhat different at the same place that today inspires him. His work appears around the world. Besides his reprint of his 2012 book *Beautiful Agitation*, also scheduled for 2020 release is *New and Selected Poems: Bones Molder, Words Hold.*

LC Gutierrez is a product of many places in the southern USA and the Caribbean, as well as writing and comparative literature programs at LSU and Tulane University (PhD). An erstwhile academic, he now writes and plays trombone in Madrid, Spain.

Lenora Rain-Lee Good lives by the Columbia River in Richland, WA. Her poetry has most recently appeared in Quill and Parchment, Ekphrastic Review, and her historical collection, Blood on the Ground: Elegies for Waiilatpu. Favorite Heinlein quote: "A poet who reads his verse in public may have other nasty habits."

Mark Tulin's books include *Magical Yogis, Awkward Grace, The Asthmatic Kids and Other Stories, Junkyard Souls*. He is a Pushcart nominee, and his work appears in *Amethyst Review, Strands Publishers, Fiction on the Web, Terror House Magazine, Beatnik Cowboy, Ariel Chart, Dreams in Fiction, Still Point Journal, The Writing Disorder,* and others. A poetry publisher compared his writing to the artist, Edward Hopper, on how he grasps unusual aspects of people and their lives. Mark is a retired psychotherapist who lives in Ventura, California with his wife, Alice. Follow him at www.crowonthewire.com, Twitter: @Crow_writer.

Mary Anne Zammit : "I am from Malta and graduate in Social Work, Probation Services, Diplomatic Studies and Masters in Probation,. I am also artist and writer and have participated in various exhibitions both locally and Internationally. I have published four novels and my poems have been featured in various editions of poetry and Anthologies."

Maya Daneva is a senior scientific staff member of the University of Twente's Services, Cybersecurity and Safety Research Group. She's a specialist in requirements engineering, effort estimation of large systems, and empirical software engineering. Previously, she spent nine years as a business process analyst in the Architecture Group at Telus. Daneva received a PhD in computer science and software engineering from St. Clement Ochridsky University.

Michael H. Brownstein's latest volume of poetry, How Do We Create Love?, was recently released (Cholla Needles Press, 2019).

Michael J. Shepley: "I am a writer.researcher in Sacramento, CA usa. My short fiction has appeared in/@ Verdad, Snail Mail Review, London Magazine & MAP with and Xmas tale to come soon in Evening Street Review."

Moshé Liba, 1931, former diplomat, lecturer, journalist, poet, writer, literary critic, painter, sculptor. Has represented the State of Israel for 31 years as Ambassador and Consul General in 15 countries. Was Director General of the Central Institute of Cultural Relations, Director of the School of Diplomats, and Director of the African Department, in the Ministry of Foreign Affairs. Is Docteur en Droit International de l''Université de Paris.Was Professor in four universities in Israel, Cameroon and New Zealand. Member of the Hebrew Writers Association in Israel, of the Haagse Kunstkring-The Netherlands, and of various other national and international associations, has lectured and published and is included in anthologies. Contributes regularly to literary, historical and international publications, reviews, periodicals, yearbooks, anthologies, and On-line publications in the Internet. Writing in several languages, has published 74 books of history, international relations, short stories, essays, literary criticism, children's books, theater-plays, albums, between them 37 books of poetry-including bilinguals and multi-linguals.Is included in the "Poetry Archive of New Zealand", has been translated in many languages, published in various countries, and awarded many honorary titles. A play in Hebrew on the basis of his book:" The Fiddler from Auschwitz" was staged in Israel in 1989. A play on the same theme written in Dutch was staged in The Hague in 2008 and in 2010.The Israeli radio station Galey Tzahal has broadcast on prime time a program about him on the national Day of the Holocaust 2012. The actress Tatiana Radier has included his poems in a Program for the Remembrance Day about children in WWII. The renowned composer Leon Biriotti (Uruguay) has composed the classical Concert: "Cinco Canciones Trágicas", on some of Liba's poems, performed as a "World Premiere" in Jerusalem in 2012.Moshé Liba is member of various national and international associations of painters and sculptors. Has been on the board of the New Zealand Academy of Fine Arts (2000-2004), and of other associations. Has presented 49 solo exhibitions and has participated in more than 300 group exhibitions;

has won various awards and recognitions. As a board member of IMAS, he is in charge of the itinerary of the "Bible Miniature Art Exhibition", touring Europe. His paintings served as scenery background for the French film "Le Grand Pardon 2", Alexandre Films, Paris, 1993. His paintings, sculptures, statues and murals are in public institutions, ministry buildings, national and city archives, libraries, museums, art galleries and private collections throughout the world. His artworks are represented in albums, anthologies, Internet websites.

Nicholas M. Sola is from LA, USA.

Nina Rubinstein Alonso: "My work has appeared in Ploughshares, The New Yorker, Ibbetson Street, Writing in a Woman's Voice, etc., and David Godine Press published my book This Body. Recent Stories were in Peacock Literary Journal and Broadkill Review. My chapbook Riot Wake is upcoming from Cervena Barva Press."

Paul Perilli: "I live in Brooklyn, NY. My fiction and nonfiction recently have been published in The Transnational, Thema, Numero Cinq, Adelaide Literary Magazine and others. My speculative fiction 'Summary Report to the Committee' appears in Overland's False Documents issue. My story 'Orwell's Year' appears as a chapbook from Blue Cubicle Press. My nonfiction travel piece 'Prices of Translation' appears in Wanderlust Journal's 2019 print anthology from Wild Dog Press. My story 'Market & Fifth, San Francisco, 1986' won the 2019 Jerry Jazz Musician short fiction contest."

Peter Hargitai: First Poet Laureate of Gulfport, Senior Lecturer, Retired Department of English, Florida International University.

Peter Magliocco writes out of Las Vegas, Nevada, where he's been active in the small press for several years as writer, poet, and artist when not editing his lit-'zine ART:MAG. A multiple nominee for the Pushcart Prize and Best of the Net, he has recent work at publications like MIDNIGHT LANE BOUTIQUE, IMPSPIRED MAGAZINE, A WORD TOO POWERFUL, GREEN SILK JOURNAL, HARBINGER ASYLUM, ARIEL CHART, and others. His latest poetry books are *Go to the Pain Lovers* (Duck Lake Books) and *The Underground Movie Poems* (Horror Sleaze Trash).

Richard Hanus: There's not much left to say. I had four kids but now have three.

Robert Malouf: Robert Malouf"I live in Wisconsin with my beloved wife, Manijeh. The simple lines I write attempt to express those promptings of the soul that well up from time to time. They originate from unexpected but welcomed insights, reflection on the more profound aspects of life, or everyday experiences."

Robert René Galván, born in San Antonio, resides in New York City where he works as a professional musician and poet. His last collection of poems is entitled, *Meteors*, published by Lux Nova Press. His poetry was recently featured in *Adelaide Literary Magazine*, *Azahares Literary Magazine*, *Gyroscope*, *Hawaii Review, Newtown Review, Panoply, Stillwater Review, West Texas Literary Review, and* the Winter 2018 issue *of UU World.* He is a Shortlist Winner Nominee in the 2018 Adelaide Literary Award for Best Poem. His poetry is included in *Undeniable: Writers Respond to Climate Change* and in *Puro ChicanX Writers of the 21st Century.*

Robin M Buehler is from NJ, USA.

Ron Riekki's most recent book is *Niiji* (co-written with Sally Brunk, Cyberwit, 2020).

Samo Kreutz is from Ljubljana, Slovenia.

Santosh Kumar (b. 1946) is a poet, short-story writer and an editor from UP India; DPhil in English; Editor of *Taj Mahal Review* and *Harvests of New Millennium* Journals; several awards; member of World Poets Society (W.P.S.); member of World Haiku Association, Japan; presented papers in the seminar, interviews as special guest at international literary festival WORDS – one path to peace and understanding Oslo, Norway in September 2008; attended 20th Annual International Literary Festival *Druskininkai Poetic Fall* and 5th World Haiku Association Conference in Lithuania, Sept 30 to Oct 5, 2009; published poetry in *Indian Verse by Young Poets (1980), World Poetry* (1995 & 1996), *The Fabric of A Vision* (2001), *The Still Horizon* (2002), *The Golden Wings* (2002), *Voyages* (2003), *Symphonies* (2003), *New Pegasus* (2004), *Explorers* (2004), *Dwan* (USA), *Promise (Purple Rose Publications, USA), World Haiku 2008 No. 4, World Haiku 2009 No. 5, Taj Mahal Review* (2002, 2003, 2004, 2005, 2006, 2007 & 2008). He has also edited sixteen World Poetry Anthologies, and four books of World's Great Short Stories. He is also the author of a collection of poems entitled *Helicon* (Cyberwit, India, ISBN 81-901366-8-2), Haiku collection *New Utopia* (Rochak Publishing, India ISBN 978-81-903812-0-8), *NO NUKES: Brave New World of Beauty, A Long Narrative Poem, Songs of Peace & Haiku* (Rochak Publishing, India ISBN 978-81-903812-3-9), and *Critical Essays* in collaboration with Adam Donaldson Powell (Cyberwit, India, 978-81-8253-110-9). He has also edited *The Poetic Achievement of Ban'ya Natsuishi* (Cyberwit, India, ISBN: 978-81-8253-149-9). His another book of literary criticism is entitled *Adam Donaldson Powell: the Making of a Poet* (Cyberwit, India, ISBN: 978-81-8253-163-5). His other books include The Haiku of *Sayumi Kamakura: A Critical Study*, and *Haiku of the Present.*

Scarlett Cunningham, Ph.D. is from AL, USA.

Steve Mogg lives in Southampton, England, and has several stories published in Scribble Magazine. He was a prize winner with 'Grace' at the 2006 Annual Writer's Conference, Winchester, England, which was published in the June 2008 issue of Taj Mahal Review. Between December 2008 and June 2019 he has also had published in Taj Mahal Review a further 23 short stories. He currently has stories on the ABC Tales website. http://www.abctales.com/user/stevem He also organises the Southern Area Chapter of the Romantic Novelists' Association.

Steve Morris teaches mathematics and science in the UK. For a number of years in his spare time, he has written modern short stories. As well as in *Taj Mahal Review,* Steve's stories have appeared in anthologies and print magazines. In December 2011 he was awarded the *AZsacra prize* for a short story in TMR. His early stories were collected together in a collection called *In All Probability with* wide press reviews. Darker stories followed in *Jumble Tales,* and these were balanced with a revengeful karma short story collection *Out on Top* before his novel about chaos when the world's technology stops working called *Playing Havoc.* www.s-morris.co.uk

Susan Signe Morrison: Writing on topics lurking in the margins of history, novelist Susan Signe Morrison is Professor of English at Texas State University. She has published poetry in *Mothering, Presence,* and *ISLE (Interdisciplinary Studies in Literature and Environment).*

Tommy Tick is a poet, busker and traveler from Long Island, NY. He urrently resides in the Florida Keys. He holds a BA in Religious Studies from St. Francis College in Brooklyn. He has been published in *50 Haikus and The Revolution* by KoA Media. He has performed his poetry at open mics in New York City, Long Island, Boston, North Carolina, Florida and New Mexico.

Victoria Crawford and George R. Ross met several years ago in a poetry appreciation group in Chiang Mai, Thailand and soon became writing partners. They often say, by the time a poem has been sent back and forth in email, who wrote which word or line? George is from Boston in the USA and was for many years a teacher in Costa Rica and the US. Victoria Crawford has a background in teaching and information science, but poetry was the link that drew them together. Their collaborations have appeared in Braided Way, Cold Noon, Active Muse, and Amethyst Review.

William Miller: "My eighth collection of poetry, LEE CIRCLE, was published by Shanti Arts Press in 2019. My poems have appeared in The American Poetry Review, The Southern Review, Shenandoah, Prairie Schooner and West Branch. I live and write in the French Quarter of New Orleans."

Wing Yau is a Hong Kong-born poet whose work appears or is forthcoming in Peril, Mascara Literary Review, Cordite Poetry Review, Eunoia Review, Ucity Review and more. Wing is now based in Melbourne, Australia.

Made in the USA
Columbia, SC
13 May 2021